ARCHITECTURE : DESIGN NOTEBOOK

For Karen

ARCHITECTURE : DESIGN NOTEBOOK

2nd edition

A. Peter Fawcett

(Illustrated by the author)

Routledge
Taylor & Francis Group

LONDON AND NEW YORK

Architectural
Press

Architectural Press is an imprint of Routledge
2 Park Square, Milton Park, Abingdon, Oxon OX14 4RN
711 Third Avenue, New York, NY 10017, USA

Routledge is an imprint of the Taylor & Francis Group, an informa business

First edition 1998
Second edition 2003

Notice
No responsibility is assumed by the publisher for any injury and/or damage to persons
or property as a matter of products liability, negligence or otherwise, or from any use
or operation of any methods, products, instructions or ideas contained in the material
herein. Because of rapid advances in the medical sciences, in particular, independent
verification of diagnoses and drug dosages should be made

British Library Cataloguing in Publication Data
Fawcett, A. Peter
  Architecture: design notebook – 2nd edn.
  1. Architecture design
  I. Title
  721

Library of Congress Cataloging-in-Publication Data
A catalog record for this book is available from the Library of Congress

ISBN: 978-0-7506-5669-6

For information on all Architectural Press publications
visit our webside at www.routledge.com

Transferred to Digital Print 2009

CONTENTS

1 PREAMBLE

As we enter the twenty-first century, it has become fashionable to consider architecture through a veil of literature. Such was not always the case; indeed, it could be argued that the practice of architecture has rarely been underpinned by a close correspondence with theory, and that designers have been drawn more to precedent, to seminal buildings and projects rather than to texts for a creative springboard to their fertile imaginations. This is merely an observation and not an argument against fledgling building designers adopting even the simplest of theoretical positions; nor does it deny the profound influence of a small number of seminal texts upon the development of twentieth-century architecture, for there has been a close correspondence between some of those texts and icons which emerged as the built outcome.

But even the most basic theoretical stance must be supported in turn by a few fundamental maxims which can point the inexperienced designer in the right direction towards prosecuting an acceptable architectural solution. This book, then, attempts to offer that support by not only offering some accepted maxims or design orthodoxies, but also by suggesting how they can inform crucial decisions which face the architect engaged in the act of designing. The text is non-theoretical and therefore makes no attempt to add to the ample literature surrounding architectural theory; rather it aims to provide students engaged in building design with a framework of accepted ways of looking at things which will support and inform their experiment and exploration during the so-called 'design process'.

The plethora of literature concerned with the 'design process' or 'design methodology' is a fairly recent phenomenon which gained momentum during the late 1950s. In these early explorations design was promulgated as a straightforward linear process from analysis via synthesis to evaluation as if conforming to some universal sequence of decision-making. Moreover, design theorists urged designers to delay as long as possible the creative leap into 'form-making' until every aspect of the architectural problem was thought to be clearly understood. But every practising architect knew that this restrictive linear model of the design process flew in the face of all shared experience; the reality of designing did not conform to a predetermined sequence at all but demanded that the designer should skip between various aspects of the problem in any order or at any time, should consider several aspects simultaneously or, indeed, should revisit some aspects in a cyclical process as the problem became more clearly defined. Furthermore, the experience of most architects was that a powerful visual image of their embryonic solution had already been formed early on in the design process, suggesting that fundamental aspects of 'form-making' such as how the building would look, or how its three-dimensional organisation would be configured in plan and section represented in reality an early, if tentative, creative response to any architectural problem.

The act of designing clearly embraces at its extremes logical analysis on the one hand and profound creative thought on the other, both of which contribute crucially to that central ground of 'form-making'. It is axiomatic that all good buildings depend upon sound and imaginative decisions on the part of the designer at these early stages and how such decision-making informs that creative 'leap' towards establishing an appropriate three-dimensional outcome.

These initial forays into 'form-making' remain the most problematic for the novice and the experienced architect alike; what follows are a few signposts towards easing a fledgling designer's passage through these potentially rough pastures.

2 THE CONTEXT FOR DESIGN

It's a hoary old cliché that society gets the architecture it deserves, or, put more extremely, that decadent regimes will, *ipso facto*, produce reactionary architecture whilst only democracies will support the progressive. But to a large extent post-Versailles Europe bore this out; the Weimar Republic's fourteen-year lifespan coincided exactly with that of the Bauhaus, whose progressive aims it endorsed, and modern architecture flourished in the fledgling democracy of Czechoslovakia. But the rise of totalitarianism in inter-war Europe soon put an end to such worthy ambition and it was left to the free world (and most particularly the New World) to prosecute the new architecture until a peaceful Europe again prevailed.

This is, of course, a gross over-simplification but serves to demonstrate that all architects work within an established socio-political framework which, to a greater or lesser extent, inevitably encourages or restricts their creative impulses, a condition which would not necessarily obtain with some other design disciplines like, for example, mechanical engineering (which, incidentally, thrived under totalitarianism).

This brings us to another well-worn stance adopted by progressive architects; that architecture (unlike mechanical engineering) responds in some measure to a prevailing cultural climate in which it is created and therefore emerges inevitably as a cultural artefact reflecting the nature of that culture. Certainly the development of progressive architecture during its so-called 'heroic' period after the First World War would seem to support this claim; architects found themselves at the heart of new artistic movements throughout Europe like, for example, Purism in Paris, De Stijl in Rotterdam, Constructivism in Moscow or the Bauhaus in Weimar and Dessau. Inevitably, such movements generated a close correspondence between architecture and the visual arts so that architects looked naturally to painters and sculptors for inspiration in their quest for developing new architectural forms. Indeed, Le Corbusier applied the formal principles of 'regulating lines' as an ordering device both to his Purist paintings and as a means subsequently of ordering the elevations to his buildings (**Figures 2.1, 2.2**). Equally, Piet Mondrian's abstract painterly compositions found themselves reinterpreted directly as three-dimensional artefacts in the architectural projects of Van Eesteren and Van Doesburg (**Figures 2.3, 2.4**), and Lubetkin's iconic Penguin Pool at London Zoo was informed by the formal explorations of Russian Constructivist sculptors like Naum Gabo (**Figures 2.5, 2.6**).

But the architectural culture of the twentieth century was also characterised by a series of

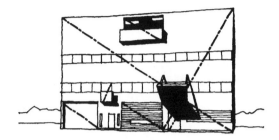

Figure 2.2 *Le Corbusier, Regulating Lines: Villa at Garches, 1927. Author's interpretation.*

theoretical models of such clarity and seductiveness that designers have since sought to interpret them directly within their 'form-making' explorations. Such was the case with Le Corbusier's 'Five Points of the New Architecture' published in 1926 where a tradi-

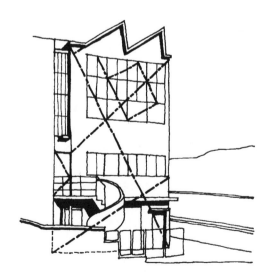

Figure 2.1 *Le Corbusier, Regulating lines, Ozenfant Studio, Paris, 1922. Author's interpretation.*

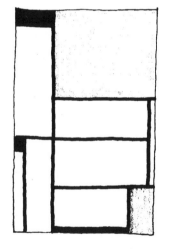

Figure 2.3 *Piet Mondrian, Tableau, 1921. From De Stijl 1917–31: Visions of Utopia, Friedman, M. (ed.), Phaidon.*

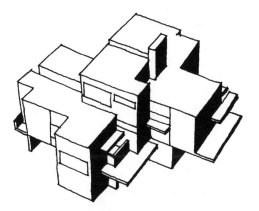

Figure 2.4 *Theo Van Doesburg and Cornelius van Eesteren, Design for house 1923 (not executed). From* De Stijl, *Overy, P., Studio Vista.*

Figure 2.6 *Naum Gabo, Construction, 1928. From* Circle, *Martin, J. L. et al. (eds), Faber and Faber.*

Figure 2.5 *Berthold Lubetkin, Penguin Pool, London Zoo, 1934. From* Berthold Lubetkin, *Allan, J., RIBA Publications.*

tional cellular domestic plan limited by the constraints of traditional timber and masonry construction was compared (unfavourably) with the formal and spatial potential afforded by reinforced concrete construction (**Figures 2.7, 2.8**). Consequently 'pilotis', 'free façade', 'open plan', 'strip window', and 'roof garden' (the five points) were instantly established as tools for form-making. A celebrated series of houses around Paris designed by Le Corbusier between 1926 and 1931 gave equally seductive physical expression to the 'five points' idea and in turn was to provide a collective iconic precedent (**Figure 2.9**). Similarly, Louis Kahn's theoretical construct of 'Servant and Served' spaces found an

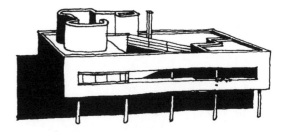

Figure 2.9 *Le Corbusier, Villa Savoye, 1931. From student model, Nottingham University.*

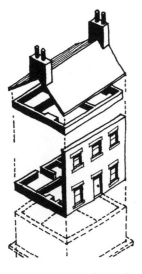

Figure 2.7 *The Five Points, Traditional House. Author's interpretation.*

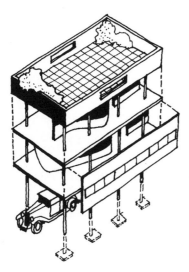

Figure 2.8 *The Five Points, Reinforced Concrete House. Author's interpretation.*

equally direct formal expression in his Richards Medical Research Building at Philadelphia completed in 1968 (**Figure 2.10**) where massive vertical shafts of brickwork enclosed the 'servant' vertical circulation and service ducts in dramatic contrast to horizontal floor slabs of the (served) laboratories and the transparency of their floor-to-ceiling glazing.

The adoption of modernism and its new architectural language was also facilitated by exemplars which were not necessarily underpinned by such transparent theoretical positions. The notion of 'precedent', therefore, has always provided further conceptual models to serve the quest for appropriate architectural forms. Such exemplars often fly in the face of orthodoxy; when Peter and Alison Smithson completed Hunstanton School, Norfolk, in 1954, they not only offered a startling 'courtyard-type' in place of the accepted Bauhaus 'finger plan' in school design (**Figures 2.11, 2.12**), but at the same time offered a new 'brutalist' architectural language as a robust

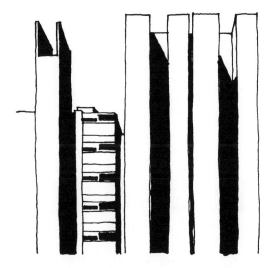

Figure 2.12   Alison and Peter Smithson, Hunstanton School, 1954. From The New Brutalism, Banham, R., Architectural Press, p. 34.

Figure 2.10   Louis Kahn, Richards Medical Research Centre, University of Pennsylvania, 1961. From Architecture Since 1945, Joedicke, J., Pall Mall.

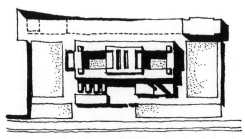

Figure 2.11   Alison and Peter Smithson, Hunstanton School, 1954. From The New Brutalism, Banham, R., Architectural Press, p. 32.

alternative to the effete trappings of the Festival of Britain.

And within this complex picture loomed a burgeoning technology which further fuelled the modernist's imagination. Architects were quick to embrace techniques from other disciplines, most notably structural and mechanical engineering and applied physics to generate new building types. The development of framed and large-span structures freed architects from the constraints of traditional building techniques where limited spans and load-bearing masonry had imposed variations on an essentially cellular plan type. Now architects could plan buildings where walls and partitions were divorced from any structural intrusion.

Whilst this revolution was facilitated by an early nineteenth-century technology, later inventions like the elevator, the electric motor and the discharge tube were to have profound effects upon a whole range of building types and therefore upon their formal outcome. For example, the elevator allowed the practical realisation of high-rise building whose potential had previously been thwarted by the limitations of the staircase (**Figure 2.13**). But the invention of the electric motor in the late nineteenth century not only facilitated the development of a cheap and practical elevator but also fundamentally changed the multi-level nineteenth-century factory type which had been so configured because of the need to harness a single source of water or steam power. The inherent flexibility of locating electric motors anywhere within the industrial process allowed the development of the single-storey deep-plan factory. Moreover, the deep-plan model applied to any building type was facilitated not only by the development of mechanical ventilation (another spin-off from the electric motor), but also by the development of the discharge tube and its application as the fluorescent tube to artificial lighting. Freed from the constraints of natural ventilation and natural lighting, architects were free to explore the formal potential of deep-plan types.

This is but a crude representation of the general milieu in which any designer operates, a context which became progressively enriched as the twentieth century unfolded. But what of the specific programme for building design which presents itself to the architect? And how do architects reconcile the generality of contextual pressures with the specific nature of, say, a client's needs, and how, in turn, are such specific requirements given formal expression?

When James Stirling designed the History Faculty Library at the University of Cambridge (completed 1968), the plan form responded directly to the client's need to prevent a spate of book theft by undergraduates. Therefore an elevated control overlooks the demi-semi-circular reading room but also the radial bookstacks, offering not only potential sec-

Figure 2.13 *Adler and Sullivan, Wainwright Building, Chicago, 1891. From* Architecture Nineteenth and Twentieth Centuries, *Hitchcock, H. R., Penguin, p. 343.*

urity for books but also a dramatic formal outcome (**Figures 2.14, 2.15**).

In 1971 Norman Foster designed an office building for a computer manufacturer in Hemel Hempstead whose principal requirement was for a temporary structure. Foster used a membrane held up by air pressure, a technique not normally applied to architecture, but which offered the potential for speedy dismantling and re-erection on another site. The translucent tent provided diffused daylighting and lamp standards were designed to give support in the event of collapse (**Figure 2.16**). Whilst this contextual 'snapshot' firmly articulates an orthodox modernist position, the so-called post-modern world has

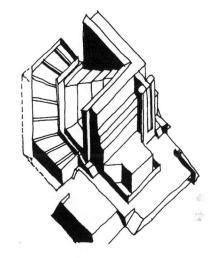

Figure 2.15   *James Stirling, History Faculty Library Cambridge, 1968, Axonometric.*

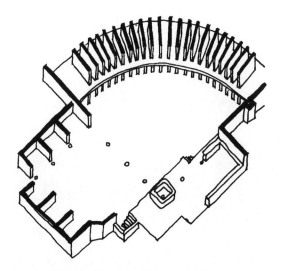

Figure 2.14   *James Stirling, History Faculty Library Cambridge, 1968, Ground floor plan.*

Figure 2.16   *Norman Foster, Computer Technology Ltd, Office, London, 1970, Section.*

offered a range of alternatives borrowed from literature and philosophy which in turn has offered architects a whole new vocabulary of form-making well removed from what many had come to regard as a doctrinaire modernist position. In this new pluralist world which revealed itself in the last quarter of the twentieth century, architects found themselves consumed by a 'freestyle' which on the one hand in revivalist mode quarried the whole gamut of architectural history (**Figure 2.17**), or on the other borrowed so-called 'de-construction' from the world of literature (**Figure 2.18**). Within this post-modern celebration of diversity, others sought a return to vernacular building forms, often applied to the most inappropriate of building types (**Figure 2.19**).

But as we enter the new millenium, deeper concerns of energy conservation and sustainability have to a large extent eclipsed the sty-

Figure 2.18 *Zaha Hadid, Kurfürstendamm, Project 1988. From* Architectural Design: Deconstruction in Architecture.

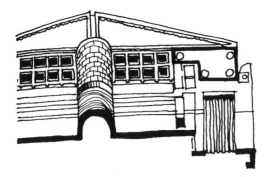

Figure 2.17 *John Outram, Terrace of Factories, 1980. From* Architectural Design: Free-style Classicism.

Figure 2.19 *Robert Matthew, Johnson-Marshall and Partners, Hillingdon Town Hall, 1978.*

listic obsessions of post-modern architects. Consequently, buildings which are thermally efficient, harness solar energy, rely on natural lighting and ventilation, reflect a return to the tectonic concerns of pioneering modernists. Moreover, like their modernist forebears, such buildings offer a fresh potential for form-making, always the primary concern of any architect (**Figure 2.20**).

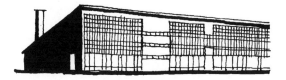

Figure 2.20 *Emslie Morgan, St Georges School, Wallasey, 1961. From* The Architecture of the Well-tempered Environment, *Banham R., Architectural Press.*

Having briefly explored a shifting context for architectural design during the twentieth century, the whole complex process of establishing an appropriate form will be examined. Although parts of the process are identified separately for reasons of clarity, each design programme generates its own priorities and therefore a different point of departure for the designer to get under way. Moreover, the designer will have to consider much of what follows simultaneously and, indeed, reconsider partially worked-out solutions as the design progresses, so that solving even relatively simple architectural problems emerges as a complex process far removed from a simple linear model.

3 ARRIVING AT THE DIAGRAM

RESPONDING TO THE SITE

Unless you are designing a demountable temporary structure capable of erection on any site, then the nature of the site is one of the few constants in any architectural programme. Other fundamentals like, for example, the brief, or the budget may well change as the design progresses, but generally the site remains as one of the few fixed elements to which the designer can make a direct response. Just as an architect may establish quite early in the design process an 'image' of his building's organisation and appearance, so must an image for the site be constructed concurrently so that the two may interact.

Analysis and survey

An understanding of the site and its potential suggests an analytical process before the business of designing can get under way. There are obvious physical characteristics like contour and climate, for example, which may stimulate the designer's creative imagination but first it is imperative to comprehend the 'sense of place' which the site itself communicates. It is necessary therefore, to have some understanding of the locality, its history, its social structure and physical patterns or 'grain', so that the form and density of your proposed interventions are appropriate. This is best achieved by observation and sketching on site as is the less problematic recording of the site's physical characteristics. How for instance will the site's topography suggest patterns of use? Is the utility of concentrating activity on the level areas of the site overridden by concerns for maintaining mature planting or avoiding overshadowing, for example? Are gradients to be utilised in generating the sectional organisation of the building? How will the building's physical form respond to and moderate the climate? Is it important to maintain existing views from the site or will the building construct its own inward-looking prospect? How is access to the site to be effected and how can the placing of buildings on the site reduce roads and site works to a minimum whilst at the same time allowing for easy circulation of people and vehicles? How do site access points respond to an existing infrastructure of vehicular and pedestrian routes? Where are existing services to the site located?

Such a survey need not be exhaustive to prompt a designer's key site responses. These in turn will be reappraised and modified along with other decisions as the design progresses. During these initial explorations it is advisable to draw the site and outline building proposals to scale so that relative sizes of the site and major building elements may be absorbed early on in the design process. In this way it is possible even at this stage to test the validity of basic design decisions and whether there exists a fundamental harmony between the site and the proposed buildings which it is to accommodate.

This whole question of an architect's response to a specific site is best illustrated by example (**Figure 3.1**). Here is a generous south facing sloping site with mature planting within a lush western suburb of Sheffield. Dramatic distant views of the city are afforded to the south and a major road forms the site's northern boundary together with vehicular and

Figure 3.1 *Fawcett, A. Peter, House for Anaesthetist, Sheffield 1987.*

pedestrian links to local facilities. The local authority insists that all mature trees on site are retained. The initial steep gradient from the road makes vehicular penetration of the site impracticable and, in the event, undesirable, given its mature planting. The client's needs appear to be even more demanding; he wishes to retire to this house with his wife and requires to live, eat and sleep at road level, that is, on an elevated plane to the north boundary. Moreover, he wishes to store his three historic motor cars at the same level and adjacent to the road to minimise hard surfacing on site. As much as possible of the mature planting on site must be retained (it is the former garden of an adjacent nineteenth-century villa). The initial diagrammatic solution (**Figures 3.2, 3.3**) demonstrates not only how responses to the site and, for example, client's needs are interdependent, but also the need to consider simultaneously various

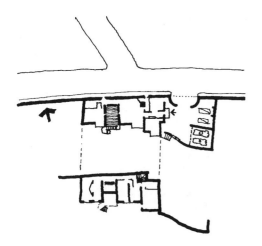

Figure 3.2 *Fawcett, A. Peter, House for Anaesthetist, Sheffield 1987, Ground floor and basement plans.*

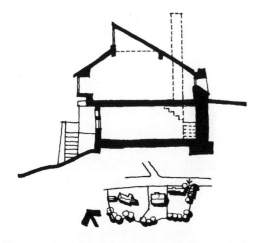

Figure 3.3 *Fawcett, A. Peter, House for Anaesthetist, Sheffield 1987, Section/site plan.*

components of the programme. Furthermore, it demonstrates how apparently severe programmatic constraints may provide a real springboard for creativity and form-making; hence the linear, single-aspect plan; the elevated living floor for access and views with service areas below; the retention of the boundary retaining wall to the north to serve also as the building's boundary thereby minimising its 'footprint' on site to preserve all mature planting; the minimal 'mews' vehicular access.

Intervention

This demonstrates how aspects of a specific programme can interact with a site to determine an optimum formal outcome. But exemplars have also conditioned architects' responses to the site during this century; these have taken on extreme positions from the archetypal Corbusian model where precise geometrical building form is set up in dramatic contrast to the landscape (**Figure 3.4**), and where 'pilotis' allow the building to hover in apparent detachment from the site, to an alternative modernist orthodoxy where a building's 'organic' form is perceived as an outcrop of the site itself (**Figure 3.5**). These positions have variously been interpreted as the self-conscious designed object contributing to the landscape (**Figure 3.6**), or, as in the case of Cullinan's visitors' centres for sensitive archaeological sites, for any intervention to

Figure 3.4 *Le Corbusier, Villa and apartment block, Wessenhofsiedlung, Stuttgart, 1927. From* Visual History of Twentieth Century Architecture, *Sharp, D., Heinemann.*

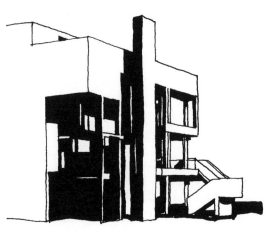

Figure 3.6 *Richard Meier, Smith House, Long Island, 1975. From* Five Architects, *Rowe, C., et al., Oxford University Press.*

Figure 3.5 *Frank Lloyd Wright Taliesin West, Arizona, 1938. From* FLW — Force of Nature, *Nash, E. P., Todtri, p. 61.*

be virtually consumed by the landscape so that physical intrusion is minimised (**Figure 3.7**).

CHOOSING AN APPROPRIATE 'MODEL'

Although it may be ill-formed and far from clear, architects generally arrive at a visual image for their building soon after the design process gets under way. Such an image often merely exists in the mind's eye long before the laborious process begins of articulating such imagery via drawings and models and then testing its validity; nevertheless, this initial creative leap into form-making, this point of

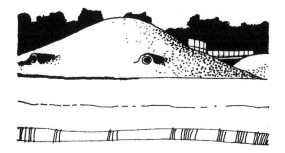

Figure 3.7 *Edward Cullinan, Archeolink Visitor Centre, Aberdeenshire, Scotland 1997. From* Architects' Journal, *6/12/97, p. 35.*

departure when the initial 'diagram' of the building begins tentatively to emerge is the most crucial and most difficult aspect of designing and, indeed, the most intimidating to a fledgling designer.

Getting started

Beaux Arts architects referred to the initial diagram of their building as the *parti*, literally, 'a point of departure'. The *parti* encapsulated the essence of a building in one simple diagram and implied that the development of the building design could proceed to completion without substantial erosion of the initial idea or *parti*. Whilst such a process had then been both informed and judged by accepted Beaux Arts canons, nevertheless the process of producing an initial diagram for a building of real clarity and order still has equal validity today even if in a pluralist modern world those canons have multiplied and shifted.

So which aspects of the 'programme' can we harness in producing this three-dimensional diagram from which the building design can evolve? What constitutes this crucial creative springboard?

As has often been articulated, architecture at its most basic manifestation is mere shelter from the elements so that human activity can be undertaken in acceptable comfort.

Should the designer assume this position, a greater concern for matters of fact rather than any theoretical stance, accepted canon, or precedent is implied. Indeed, the earliest, most primitive attempts at making shelter against the elements merely assembled available materials to hand; this was an entirely pragmatic process of design by trial and error (**Figure 3.8**). Even today, some decisions embodied in the design process are entirely pragmatic in nature particularly when incorporating new materials or methods of construction; early crude and tentative efforts tend to be refined and modified by trial and error using the same pragmatic processes as our forebears.

But in searching for this initial form or *parti* it is unlikely that purely pragmatic considerations will dominate. Designers are much more likely to be profoundly influenced by accepted ways of doing things or canons which are a useful source for ordering this notoriously problematic form-finding process. Classical architects worked, literally, within

Figure 3.8 *Guyanan benab.*

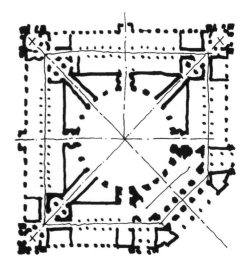

Figure 3.9 *Sir E. Cooper, Port of London Authority Building, 1931.*

the ordering device of the orders and similarly, the Beaux Arts *parti* relied on its own canonic devices which effectively ordered within an accepted framework the architect's initial forays into form-making (**Figure 3.9**). With the advent of modernism, Le Corbusier's 'Regulating Lines' and his later 'Modulor' were presented as canons based upon the same mathematical origins and with the same outcome in mind; they similarly offered a set of devices to order and clarify architectural form.

Typology

To a large extent the notion of typology (or study of 'types') has replaced the Beaux Arts

parti in more recent times as a crucial point of departure in our formal explorations. This is, of course, an over-simplification, for eighteenth- and nineteenth-century architects were deeply concerned with the idea of building 'types' classified by use, which reflected an equally profound concern on the part of contemporaneous scientists for classifying by 'type' the entire natural world.

We have already seen how pragmatic designers in their quest to develop primitive forms of shelter developed buildings which in their forms and materials were closely associated with nature; materials at hand were assembled in such a way as to meet the demands of climate and user alike. This developed into a vernacular typology (**Figure 3.10**) in which architecture and nature established a close correspondence, a source of constant inspiration to both designers and theorists since the eighteenth century. But as a burgeoning nineteenth-century technology in turn created a new building technology, so a new tectonic typology (**Figure 3.11**) emerged concerned with new structural and constructional devices far removed from vernacular precedent. Finally, architects have found themselves profoundly influenced by the physical context in which they design, so that a contextual typology (**Figure 3.12**) has developed. Not surprisingly, all these typologies have been developed to great levels of sophistication and represent, as a combined resource in the form of exemplary precedent, the fundamental springboard for effectively prosecuting building design.

Figure 3.11   *Contamin et Dutert, Palais des Machines, Paris Exposition, 1889. From* Space, Time and Architecture, *Gideon, S., Oxford University Press, p. 270.*

Figure 3.12   *Robert Venturi, Sainsbury Wing, National Gallery, London, 1991. From* A Celebration of Art and Architecture, *Amery, C., National Gallery, p. 106.*

Figure 3.10   *Vernacular, Barns, Suffolk.*

Plan type

So much for a broad perspective of typologies as another backdrop to creative activity, but how can we harness specific typologies to help us develop our building as a three-dimensional artefact? Le Corbusier famously declared, 'The plan is the generator'; putting aside for a moment that much meaning was lost in the English translation ('the three-dimensional organisation is the generator' would have been nearer the mark) it nevertheless suggests that plan types can indeed provide one of many departure points (others will be discussed later). Further putting aside whether your building will adhere to free or geometric forms, or both, it is still possible to distil a remarkably limited range of basic plan types which tend to be variations on linear, courtyard, linked pavilion, shed, or deep-plan organisations (**Figures 3.13–3.17**). There are, of course, massive variations on each type and most buildings combine aspects of more than one to satisfy the needs of a complex brief. Nevertheless, this initial stab at establishing a plan form which will provide an appropriate 'frame' to sustain specific social activities, is one crucial decision which allows the design to proceed.

Building type

Historically, of course, plan types like, for example, the 'basilica' or 'rotunda' were

Figure 3.13   *Barry Johns, Technology Centre, Edmonton, 1987. From* Architectural Review, *May 1987, p. 82.*

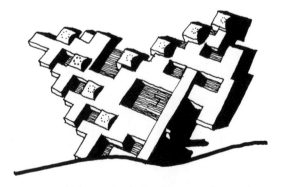

Figure 3.14   *Aldo Van Eyck, Orphanage, Amsterdam, 1960. From* The New Brutalism, *Banham, R., Architectural Press, p. 158.*

Figure 3.15   *Eiermann and Ruf, West German Pavilion, World's Fair, Brussels, 1958. From* A Visual History of Twentieth Century Architecture, *Sharp, Heinemann, p. 223.*

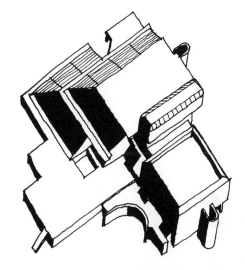

Figure 3.17   *Ahrends, Burton and Karolek, Portsmouth Polytechnic Library, 1979. From ABK,* Architectural Monograph, Academy Editions, *p. 99.*

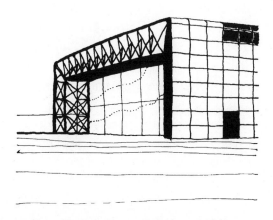

Figure 3.16   *Norman Foster, Sainsbury Building, University of East Anglia, 1977.*

often closely associated with specific building types and this linkage between plan and building type has, if less dogmatically, nevertheless still persisted in characterising twentieth-century architecture also (**Figures 3.18, 3.19**). But inevitably such orthodoxies are challenged from time to time and these challenges are generally recorded as important catalysts in architectural development.

Thus the linked pavilion type of post-war school buildings in Britain was challenged by the Smithsons in 1949 at Hunstanton School where a courtyard type was adopted (**Figure 3.20**), but also by Greater London Council Architects' Department in 1972 at Pimlico

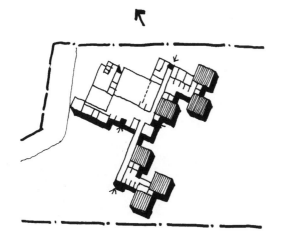

Figure 3.18 *C. Aslin, County Architect, Hertfordshire, Aboyne Infants School, 1949.*

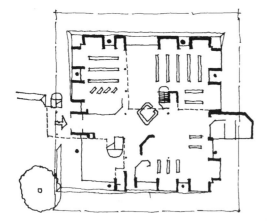

Figure 3.19 *Ahrends, Burton and Koralek, Maidenhead Library, 1972. From ABK,* Architectural Monograph, *Academy Editions, p. 65.*

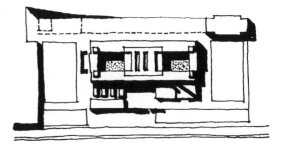

Figure 3.20 *Alison and Peter Smithson, Hunstaton School, 1954. From* The New Brutalism, *Banham, R., Architectural Press.*

School where a linear plan type not only responded to its London square context but also to the notion of an internal 'street' where informal social contact could take place (**Figure 3.21**).

Similarly, pressures to conserve energy by utilising natural ventilation and lighting led Michael Hopkins to adopt a narrow plan for his Inland Revenue offices in Nottingham in 1995 (**Figure 3.22**). This has been configured within a courtyard type effectively replacing the established deep-plan orthodoxy of the office type which the development of mechanical ventilation and permanent artificial lighting (both high energy consumers) had facilitated. Moreover, the courtyard has generated an acceptable urban form with a public domain of tree-lined boulevards and a private domain of enclosed courts (**Figure 3.23**). Consequently, Hopkins has capitalised on one severe constraint not only to challenge an accepted

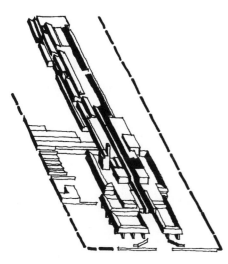

Figure 3.21 *John Bancroft (GLC Architects' Department), Pimlico Secondary School, 1966. From* Architectural Review 1/66, p. 31.

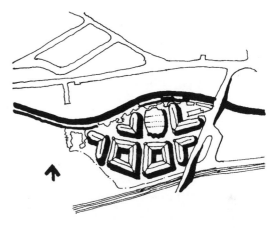

Figure 3.23 *Sir Michael Hopkins and Partners, Inland Revenue Offices, Nottingham, 1995. Site plan. From* Architectural Review 5/95, p. 34.

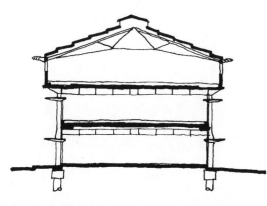

Figure 3.22 *Sir Michael Hopkins and Partners, Inland Revenue Offices, Nottingham, 1995. Section. From* Architectural Review 5/95, p. 34.

office type, but has also been able to offer a model at an urban scale for controlling the chaotic growth of our cities.

ORGANISING THE PLAN

As the building design develops from the initial diagram, it is essential on the one hand to maintain the clarity of that diagram and on the other to keep testing its validity as the architectural problem itself is clarified so that the *parti* is constantly revisited for reappraisal. This whole process of establishing in detail the building's three-dimensional organisation is best explored through the medium of drawing; a facility for drawing in turn facilitates designing in that ideas can be constantly (and quickly) explored and evaluated for inclusion in the design, or rejected.

Many commentators have argued that the problematic process of form-making can be rooted in drawing, and more specifically, within established techniques. This has been suggested in the case of James Stirling's most celebrated works from the 1960s, the Engineering Building, Leicester, 1964, and the History Faculty Library, Cambridge, 1968, where, arguably, the formal outcome has to some extent been a product of an axonometric drawing method (**Figures 3.24, 3.25**). This may seem a far-fetched proposi-

tion, for clearly these buildings are rooted in traditions which transcend any concerns for drawing technique; the nineteenth-century functional tradition and the modernist tradition.

Thus, we have two buildings which, in their formal outcome, express a fundamental canon of modernism; that a building's three-dimensional organisation (and functional planning) should be clearly expressed as overt display. Hence the separate functions of workshop, laboratory and lecture theatre are clearly and distinctly articulated at Leicester as are the functions of reading room and bookstack at Cambridge.

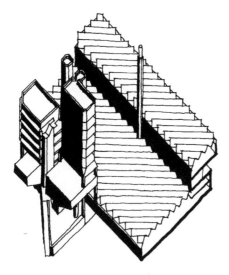

Figure 3.24 *James Stirling, Leicester Engineering Building, Leicester University, 1964, Second floor plan. From* Architectural Design, *2/64, p. 69.*

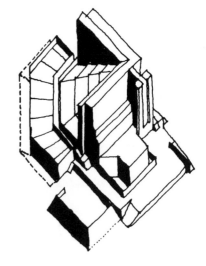

Figure 3.25 *James Stirling, History Faculty, Cambridge, 1968. From* Architectural Review, *11/68, p. 330.*

Circulation

But apart from expressing an organisation of disparate functional parts, Stirling's three-dimensional models express ideas about circulation within the building (**Figures 3.26, 3.27**). Indeed, concern for imparting some formal expression to horizontal and vertical circulation systems within buildings has constantly been an overriding concern to architects of modernist persuasion. Hence the obsession with free-standing stair towers and lift shafts which connect by landing and bridge to the principal building elements, and the equally strong desire to express major horizontal circulation systems within the building envelope.

Indeed, many architects think of circulation routes as 'armatures' upon which cells of accommodation are hung (**Figure 3.28**) so that expressing circulation patterns not only becomes central to establishing a functional working plan but also in turn gives authori-

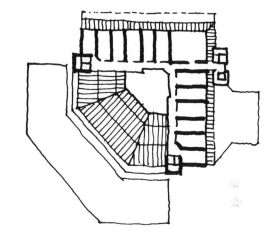

Figure 3.27   *History Faculty, Cambridge, 1968, Fifth floor plan. From* Architectural Review, *11/68, p. 337.*

tative clues to the form-finding process. Moreover, attitudes towards circulation can modify and enrich basic plan types. For example, whether a linear building is configured as single or dual aspect will affect the plan and therefore the formal outcome (**Figure 3.29**). Similarly, a 'racetrack' circulation route within a courtyard building may be internal (**Figure 3.30**) or may be shifted laterally to relate directly to the internal court (**Figure 3.31**); clearly, such decisions concerning circulation within buildings not only affect the nature of principal internal spaces but in the case of a courtyard type, the nature of the courtyard itself. Should this model be developed further into the so-called 'atrium' plan then the

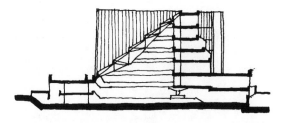

Figure 3.26   *James Stirling, History Faculty, Cambridge, 1968. From* Architectural Review, *11/68, p. 337.*

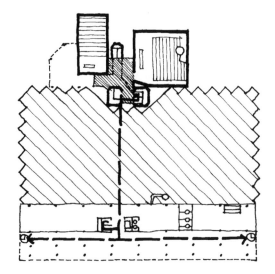

Figure 3.28 *James Stirling, Leicester Engineering Building, Leicester University, 1964, Second floor plan. From* Architectural Review, *2/64, p. 66.*

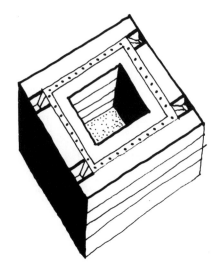

Figure 3.30 *'Race-track' courtyard plan, dual aspect.*

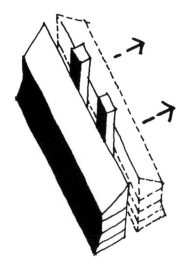

Figure 3.29 *Linear plan, single/dual aspect.*

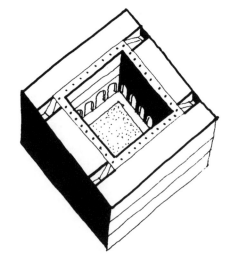

Figure 3.31 *'Race-track' courtyard plan, single aspect.*

atrium, or covered courtyard, will itself assume a circulation role (**Figure 3.32**).

Unless the 'architectural promenade' is to be celebrated as a means of clarifying the building's organisation (this will be discussed later), there will be pressure on the designer to minimise circulation routes. Clearly, this pursuit presents some difficulties when faced with a linear building, but there are devices which an architect can use to minimise the apparent length of the inevitable corridors and galleries which result from such a type.

Horizontal circulation

Essentially, such devices will serve to punctuate these routes by variations in lighting, for example, which may well correspond to 'nodes'

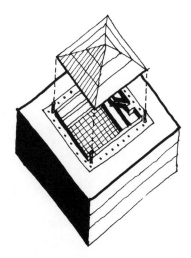

Figure 3.32 *'Atrium' courtyard plan.*

along the route like lobbies for vertical circulation (**Figure 3.33**). Further punctuations of the route can be achieved by 'sub-spaces' off the major route which mark the access points to cellular accommodation within the building (**Figure 3.34**). Such 'sub-spaces' may also provide a useful transition between the route or concourse, and major spaces within the building.

Circulation routes also have an important role in helping us to 'read' buildings. First, there is a hierarchy of routes in any building and this can be used to clarify the functional plan so that diagrammatically, patterns of circulation are tree-like with primary concourse (trunk) and secondary corridors (branches) (**Figure 3.35**). But it is also essential that these routes are punctuated by events which also help us to 'read' the building's three-dimensional organisation. Reiterated references to major events within the building also help the user to 'read' and comprehend the functional plan; these 'structuring points' may be nodes of vertical circulation or major public spaces like foyers, concourses, or auditoria (**Figure 3.36**). Patterns of circulation also allow us to orientate ourselves within the plan by not only engaging with major internal events, but also with those outside; views out onto the site or into courtyards provide a constant reference to the user for purposes of orientation.

Figure 3.33 *Route 'node'.*

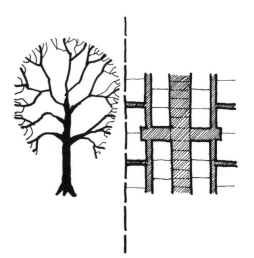

Figure 3.35 *Tree/circulation analogy.*

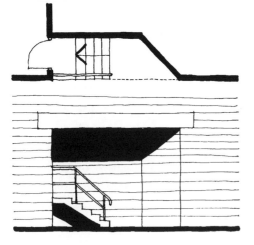

Figure 3.34 *'Sub-space' off circulation route, plan/ elevation.*

Figure 3.36 *Herman Hertzberger, Ministry of Social Affairs, The Hague, 1990. Upper floor plan.*

Vertical circulation

The location of vertical circulation also contributes substantially to this idea of 'reading' a building and clearly is crucial in evolving a functional plan. There is also a hierarchy of vertical circulation; service or escape stairs, for example, may be discreetly located within the plan so as not to challenge the primacy of a principal staircase (**Figure 3.37**).

Moreover, a stair or ramp may have other functions besides that of mere vertical circulation; it may indicate the principal floor level or *piano nobile* where major functions are accommodated, or may be a vehicle for dramatic formal expression (**Figure 3.38**).

And what form should the stair or ramp take? A dog-leg stair or ramp allows the user to re-engage with the same location on plan from floor to floor (**Figure 3.39**), whilst a running or straight flight configuration (including the escalator) implies vertical movement within some horizontal 'promenade' so that the user alights at different locations on plan (**Figure 3.40**) at each floor level. Should the stair or ramp be curved on plan, then a further dynamic element is introduced (**Figure 3.41**). Landings may not only punctuate flights, but if generous enough, may induce social contact as informal meeting places.

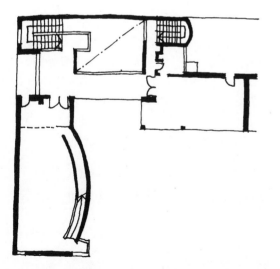

Figure 3.37 *Le Corbusier, Maison La Roche, 1923. First floor plan. From student model, Nottingham University.*

Figure 3.38 *Alvar Aalto, Institute of Pedagogics, Jyvaskyala, Finland, 1957. From* Alvar Aalto 1898–1976, Museum of Finnish Architecture, *p. 75.*

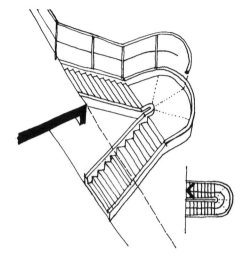

Figure 3.39 *'Dog-leg' stair.*

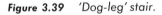

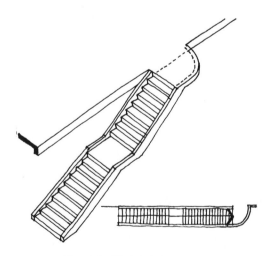

Figure 3.40 *'Straight-flight' stair.*

Figure 3.41 *Le Corbusier, Maison La Roche, 1923.*

The promenade

Closely associated with any strategy for circulation within a building is the notion of 'promenade' or 'route'. This implies an understanding of buildings via a carefully orchestrated series of sequential events or experiences which are linked by a predetermined route. How the user approaches, enters and then engages with a building's three-dimensional organisation upon this 'architectural promenade' has been a central pursuit of architects throughout history.

The external stair, podium, portico and vestibule were all devices which not only isolated a private interior world from the public realm outside but also offered a satisfactory spatial transition from outside to inside (**Figure 3.42**). Moreover, these devices were reiterated and reinterpreted during the twentieth century as a central modernist concern; the floating podium, often associated with water, assumes the role of a 'ceremonial bridge' (**Figure 3.43**), and the projecting canopy or deeply recessed entrance replaces the classical portico as not only 'marking' an entrance, but also by allowing some engagement with the building before entry (**Figures 3.44, 3.45**).

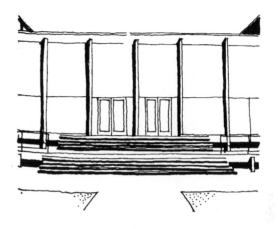

Figure 3.43 *Mies van der Rohe, Crown Hall, Illinois Institute of Technology, 1956. From* Modern Architecture since 1900, *Curtis, W., Phaidon, p. 262.*

Figure 3.42 *Bernini, Saint Andrea al Quirinale, Rome, 1678. From* The World Atlas of Architecture, *Mitchell Beazley, p. 303.*

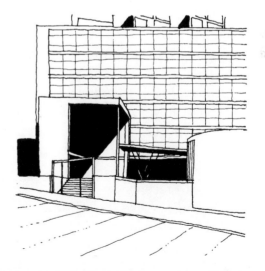

Figure 3.44 *Le Corbusier, Salvation Army, City of Refuge, Paris, 1933. From* Le Corbusier and the Tragic View, *Jenkins, C., Allen Lowe, p. 116.*

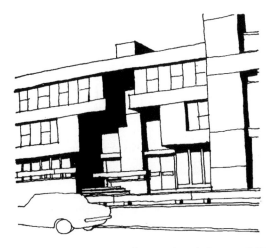

Figure 3.45 *Peter Womersley, Roxburgh County Offices, 1968*

The exemplar

By the late 1920s Le Corbusier had developed the notion of *promenade architecturale* to a very high level of sophistication. At the Villa Stein, Garches, 1927, a carefully orchestrated route not only allows us to experience a complex series of spaces but also by aggregation gives us a series of clues about the building's organisation. The house is approached from the north and presents an austere elevation with strip windows like an abstract 'purist' painting. But the elevation is relieved by devices which initiate our engagement with the building. The massively-scaled projecting canopy 'marks' the major entrance and relegates the service entrance to a secondary role.

At the same time the two entrances are differentiated by size thereby removing any hint of duality or ambiguity (**Figure 3.46**), and a pierced opening in the parapet suggests the existence of a roof terrace. On entry, an opening in the first floor provides a gallery which immediately asserts the importance of the first floor; the *piano nobile* has been established. A free-standing dog-leg stair allows us to re-engage directly with the void at first floor level, the serpentine edge of which invites a further exploration of the plan. Generous glazing to the south elevation engages with the garden beyond, but the pre-determined route then leads to an external terrace which, because of the complex sectional organisation involving further terraces overhead, reads as a transitional space between inside and outside. Finally, a straight-flight stair leads into a garden to conclude a complex promenade (**Figure 3.47**). The route reveals sequentially the building's principal spaces but at the same

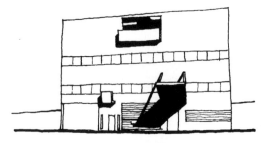

Figure 3.46 *Le Corbusier, Villa at Garches, 1927. North elevation.*

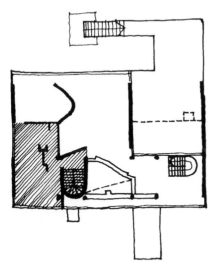

Figure 3.47 *Le Corbusier, Villa at Garches, 1927. First floor plan. From student model, University of Nottingham.*

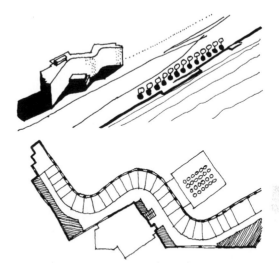

Figure 3.48 *Alvar Aalto, Baker House, Cambridge, Massachusetts, 1951. From* Modern Architecture since 1900, *Curtis, W., Phaidon, p. 297.*

time conceals the 'service' elements of the plan like service stair, servants' quarters at ground floor and kitchen at first floor to establish a clear functional hierarchy.

Whereas at Garches the route marks and celebrates the prominence of an elevated first floor or *piano nobile*, the reverse can be employed to equally dramatic effect; at Alvar Aalto's serpentine student dormitory block for Massachusetts Institute of Technology, Cambridge, Mass., 1949, visitors engage with this riverside building at high level and descend into the principal foyer and social spaces with views over the Charles River (**Figure 3.48**).

James Stirling developed this notion of a complex route within the context of a highly disciplined plan to further levels of sophistication at two celebrated art galleries; the Neue Staatsgalerie at Stuttgart, 1984 (**Figure 3.49**), and the Clore Gallery, Tate Gallery, London, 1986 (**Figure 3.50**). Both celebrate access by preamble and transition and both buildings use the promenade as a powerful structuring device engaging with ramps and stairs which provide a dynamic element alongside a controlled sequence of gallery spaces.

At a more prosaic level, Peter Womersley employed similar devices to describe the

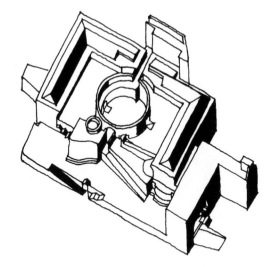

Figure 3.49 *James Stirling, Staatsgalerie, Stuttgart, 1984. From* Architectural Review, *12/92, p. 77.*

organisation of his design for Roxburgh County Offices, Scotland, 1970 (**Figure 3.51**). Here a 'campanile' forming strong-rooms at each office level initially marks but conceals from view the entrance, itself high-lighted by a deep recession within the office structure. This, in turn, gives access to an entrance foyer, also double height with over-sailing gallery at first floor. The entrance doors flank a lift shaft which is expressed externally and the foyer engages with a central court-yard. Therefore, by using such simple devices, the essence of this public building is directly revealed to the user; a three-storey courtyard typology with dual aspect cellular offices linked by a central 'racetrack' corridor.

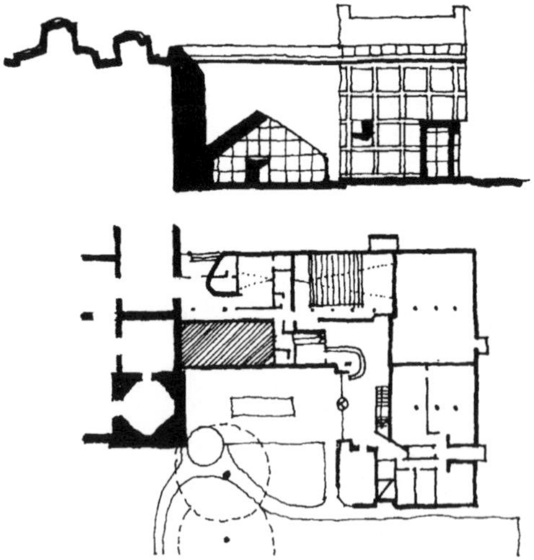

Figure 3.50 *James Stirling, Clore Gallery, Tate Gallery, London Plan, Elevation. From* A-D Freestyle Classicism, *1982, p. 108.*

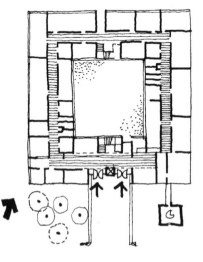

Figure 3.51 *Peter Womersley, Roxburgh County Offices, 1968, Ground floor plan.*

Whilst formally of a very different genre, Womersley nevertheless similarly harnesses the promenade to describe and clarify the fundamental components of a functional plan.

Spatial hierarchies

Whilst such patterns of circulation and the ordering of 'routes' through a building allow us to 'read' and to build up a three-dimensional picture, there remains the equally important question of how we communicate the essential differences between the spaces which these systems connect. This suggests a hierarchical system where spaces, for example, of deep symbolic significance, are clearly identified from run-of-the-mill elements which merely service the architectural programme so that an organisational hierarchy is articulated via the building. Similarly, for example, when designing for the community it is essential that those spaces within the public domain are clearly distinguished from those deemed to be intensely private. Between these two extremes there is, of course, a range of spatial events which needs to be placed within this hierarchical order which the building also must communicate.

This clear distinction was achieved by Denys Lasdun at the Royal College of Physicians, Regent's Park, London, 1960 (**Figure 3.52**), where the ceremonial area of the building addresses the park as a stark stratified pavilion

Figure 3.52 *Denys Lasdun, Royal College of Physicians, London, 1959. From* Denys Lasdun, *Curtis, W., Phaidon.*

elevated on *pilotis*. By contrast, the office element is expressed simply as a self-effacing infill to the street beyond (**Figure 3.53**). Moreover, the distinction is clearly expressed externally and further reinforced as the plan is explored internally.

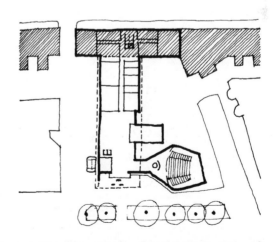

Figure 3.53 *Denys Lasdun, Royal College of Physicians, London, 1959. From* Denys Lasdun, *Curtis, W., Phaidon.*

Sub-spaces

This whole question of spatial hierarchy may also be applied to sub-spaces which are sub-servient to a major spatial event like side chapels relating to the major worship space within a church. At the monastery of La Routette, Eveux-sur-Arbresle, France, 1959, Le Corbusier contrasted the stark dimly-lit cuboid form of the church with brightly-lit side chapels of sinuous plastic form which were further highlighted by the application of primary colour against the grey *béton brut* of the church (**Figure 3.54**). Such a juxtaposition served to heighten not only the architectural drama but also the primacy of the principal worship space.

Although using a different architectural vocabulary, C. R. Mackintosh sought similarly to clarify a major space (bedroom) at Hill House, Helensburgh, Scotland, 1904, which associated sub-spaces enriched rather than challenged (**Figure 3.55**). But the means were the same; by means of a taller ceiling and a simple rectilinear geometry, the major space retains its dominance.

Similarly, public buildings like theatres must establish a clear distinction between public and private domains of 'front' and 'back' of house. Lasdun's National Theatre, London, 1976, articulates this distinction through external architectural expression, but more directly by means of a clear planning strategy which is

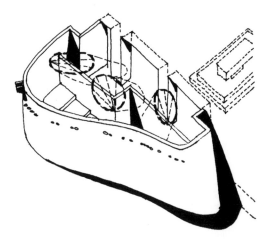

Figure 3.54 *Le Corbusier, Monastery of La Tourette, Eveux, 1955.*

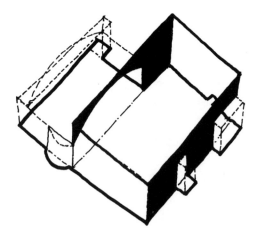

Figure 3.55 *C. R. Mackintosh, Hill House, Helensburgh, Scotland, 1903. Main bedroom.*

immediately comprehensible (**Figure 3.56**) and avoids any hint of ambiguity.

Inside-outside

Establishing and then articulating these spatial hierarchies within the context of a functional plan has exercised architects throughout history; a system of axes employed by Beaux Arts architects, for example, greatly facilitated this pursuit. But many architects of modernist persuasion, in their desire to break with tradition, have shed such ordering devices and have espoused the liberating potential that developments in abstract art and building technology seemed to offer. One outcome was functional planning freed from the formality of symmetry and axiality (**Figure 3.57**) but another was a concern for establishing an almost seamless relationship between inside and outside spaces. This allowed the designer to punctuate the plan with external spaces which were expressed as internal spaces without a roof. Moreover, the development of glazed curtain walls as movable screens allowed the complete correspondence between outside and inside uninterrupted by major structural intrusion.

Even by the mid-1920s modernists had developed such techniques to a remarkable level of sophistication; Le Corbusier's Parisian villas at Garches, 1927, and Poissy, 1931, deploy controlled external spaces as an

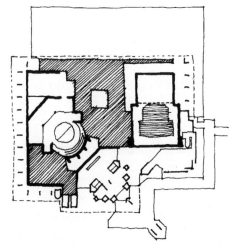

Figure 3.56 *Denys Lasdun, National Theatre, London, Plan. From* Denys Lasdun, *Curtis, W., Phaidon.*

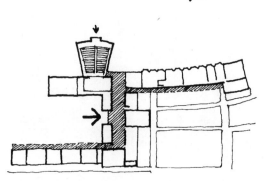

Figure 3.57 *Walter Gropius and Maxwell Fry, Impington College, Cambridge, England, 1936, Plan. From* Walter Gropius, *Berdini, P., Gustavo Gilli, Barcelona, p. 155.*

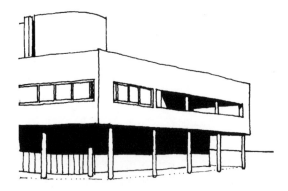

Figure 3.60   *Le Corbusier, Villa Savoye, Poissy, 1929.*

Figure 3.58   *Le Corbusier, Villa at Garches, 1927. From* L'Architecture Vivante, *Le Corbusier, Albert Moranc.*

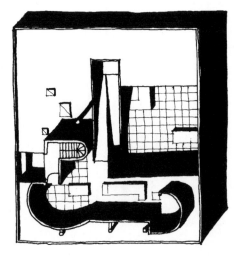

Figure 3.59   *Le Corbusier, Villa Savoye, Poissy, 1929. From student model,* University of Nottingham.

extension of habitable rooms. At Garches full-height parapet walls punctuated by carefully-placed openings enclose what are in effect external living spaces (**Figure 3.58**). At Poissy an internal ramp engages with an external terrace and terminates at a solarium (**Figure 3.59**) and the *fenêtre longue* of the living room is projected into the full-height enclosing parapet of the adjacent terrace, establishing yet another inside/outside ambiguity (**Figure 3.60**).

4 CHOOSING APPROPRIATE TECHNOLOGIES

In our quest for form-making we have long been aware of the role of technology; in the eighteenth century Marc-Antoine Laugier, the celebrated critic, declared that technique was the prime cause of architectural expression, a proposition developed in the nineteenth century and indeed, adopted as a central plank of modernism in the twentieth. But the proposition has much deeper roots; primitive builders looked around them for available building materials which, when assembled, could provide shelter.

STRUCTURE

Such materials tended to be sticks, blocks, membranes (animal skins), or malleable clay which developed into an orthodoxy of framed, planar or plastic structural forms respectively (**Figures 4.1–4.3**).

Although this represents an over-simplification, nevertheless, there are several modernist icons which clearly express a similar range of structural forms apparently facilitated by a burgeoning technology. Not unnaturally, the same formal categories of framed, planara,

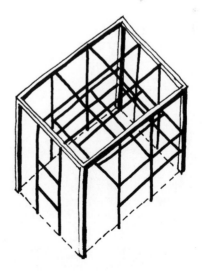

Figure 4.1 Framed form.

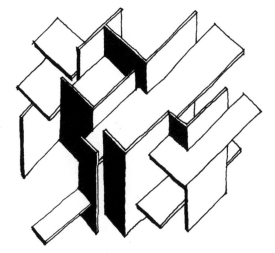

Figure 4.2   *Planar form.*

and plastic were to emerge pursued with varying degrees of rigour. Mies van der Rohe's Farnsworth House, Plano, Illinois, 1951, remains as the archetypal framed pavilion (**Figure 4.4**), Gerrit Rietveld's Schröder House, Utrecht, 1924, celebrated the potential of planar form (**Figure 4.5**), whilst Erich Mendelsohn's Einstein Tower, Pottsdam, 1924 explored plasticity (**Figure 4.6**). Whereas these examples demonstrate an adherence to one formal type, most buildings embody all three simultaneously. Le Corbusier's seminal Villa Savoye, Poissy, 1931, is a case in point; here, 'framed' pilotis support the cuboid 'planar' elements of the principal floor which in turn is surmounted by the 'plastic' forms of the solarium (**Figure 4.7**).

But such attempts to explore the potential of new building techniques in establishing a modernist formal vocabulary exposed pro-

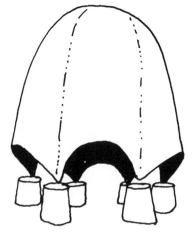

Figure 4.3   *Plastic form.*

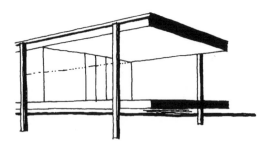

Figure 4.4   *Mies van der Rhe, Farnsworth House, Plano, Illinois, 1950. From* Architecture Since 1945, *Joedicke, J., Pall Mall, p. 89.*

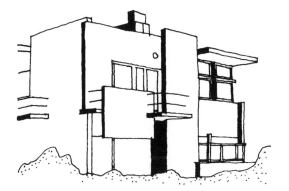

Figure 4.5 *Gerrit Rietveld, Schröder House, Utrecht, 1924. From* Visual History of Twentieth Century Architecture, *Sharp, D., Heinemann, p. 75.*

found contradictions; smooth, welded junctions in the Farnsworth House's steel frame were achieved by labour-intensive grinding, essentially a craft technique; the spectacular cantilevered roof and floor planes at the Schröder House were achieved by a pragmatic mixture of masonry, steel, and timber, suggesting that a close correspondence between form and structure was not high on the design agenda; similarly pragmatic and craft-based were the plastering techniques employed at the Einstein Tower in pursuit of plasticity, and even the smooth machine-like planes at the Villa Savoye were achieved with the help of skilled Italian plasterers.

Already discussed is the profound effect of technological invention and development upon building types and therefore form-making. Indeed, a modernist orthodoxy decreed that, 'The Modern Movement in architecture, in order to be fully expressive of the twentieth century, had to possess . . . faith in science and technology . . .' (Pevsner).

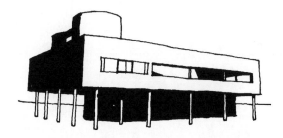

Figure 4.6 *Erich Mendelsohn, Einstein Tower, Potsdam, 1921. From* Architects' Journal 4.6, p. 64.

Figure 4.7 *Le Corbusier, Villa Savoye, Poissy, 1931. From* Le Corbusier and the Tragic View of Architecture, *Jencks, C., Penguin Allen Lane, p. 92.*

SERVICES

Consequently, architects seized upon not only the form-making potential of new structural techniques, but also that of mechanical services.

This approach reached its zenith at the Centre Georges Pompidou, Paris, 1977 (**Figure 4.8**), and at the headquarters for Lloyd's of London, 1986 (**Figure 4.9**), both by Richard Rogers, where the conventional central core of services within a flexible space was reversed so that these elements were shifted to the periphery of the building. Furthermore, they were given clear external expression so that lift cars,

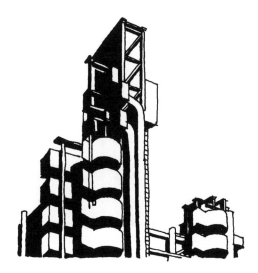

Figure 4.9 *Richard Rogers, Lloyds Building, London, 1986. From* Richard Rogers, Architectural Monographs, Academy, p. 129.

escalators, and ventilation ducts were displayed as a dramatic image of so-called 'hi-tech' architecture.

But such had not always been the case; progressive nineteenth-century architects, equally concerned with incorporating the benefits of a burgeoning technology within their buildings, felt no compulsion to express such innovation either internally or externally and it was only those architects who did so, however tentatively, that gained any credit as precursors of the modernist cause (**Figure 4.10**). Similarly, architects of so-called post-modern persuasion have also felt little compulsion to allow innovative structure or services to inform an

Figure 4.8 *Richard Rogers, Centre Georges Pompidou, Paris, 1977.*

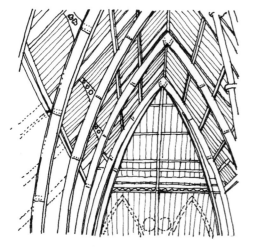

Figure 4.10 *Deane and Woodward, Museum of Natural History, Oxford, 1861. From* Bannister Fletcher, *Architectural Press, p. 1024.*

Figure 4.11 *Moore, Grover, Harper, Sammis Hall, 1981. North elevation. From* Freestyle Classicism, Jenks, C., A–D, *p. 81.*

architectural expression whose origins were quite remote from such considerations (**Figure 4.11**). The honest expression of elements which make up a building exercised architects throughout the twentieth century so that a question of morality has constantly underpinned the modernists' creed, a position joyously abandoned by their post-modern brethren.

HOW WILL IT STAND UP?

Nowhere is this notion of architectural honesty more prevalent than in structural expression. We have seen how architects have sought to

express diagrams of circulation within their buildings or have indicated a functional organisation of volumes through direct formal expression, but designers have also harnessed structure as a principal generator in their form-finding explorations.

Structural expression

The logical conclusion of this pursuit of structural expression is a close correspondence of structure, form and space enclosure. This total interdependence has been a central pursuit of modernists and accounts for their liberal references to such nineteenth-century icons as Dutert's Galerie des Machines built for the 1889 Parisian Exposition (**Figure 4.12**), or Fryssinet's airship hangars at Orly, France, 1916 (**Figure 4.13**). Where the architectural

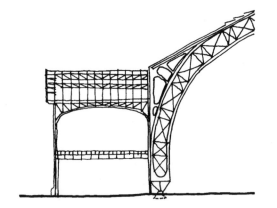

Figure 4.12 *Contamin et Dutert, Galerie des Machines, Paris Exposition, 1889. From Durant, S.,* Architecture in Detail, *Phaidon.*

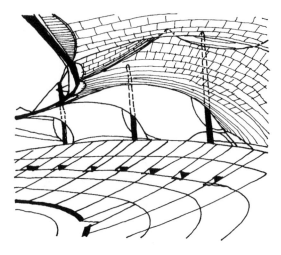

Figure 4.14 *Frei Otto, Olympic Games Complex, Munich, 1972. From* Dictionary of Architecture, *St James Press, p. 243.*

programme lends itself to such direct or 'one-liner' solutions, such as in the case of exhibition buildings, then this inseparability of form, space and structure is more likely to be realised.

This has consistently been the case with the tent-like structures of Frei Otto (**Figure 4.14**), or with the geodesic domes of Buckminster

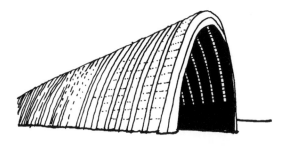

Figure 4.13 *Freyssinet, Airship Hangar, Orly, Paris, 1916. From* Bannister Fletcher, *Architectural Press, p. 1106.*

Fuller (**Figure 4.15**) where decisions about structure determine the nature of external form but also as a direct outcome, the type of space enclosed. Furthermore, the nature of the external membranes of both examples allows a close correspondence with the structure whilst at the same time providing transparency or translucency for daylighting purposes.

But such structural virtuosity, whilst a demonstration of skill admirably suited to an exhibition building where the primary need is for one large uncluttered and flexible space, is hardly appropriate for more complex architectural programmes; in such situations, the designer re-engages with the notion of 'type'. Although modern structural engineering techniques may

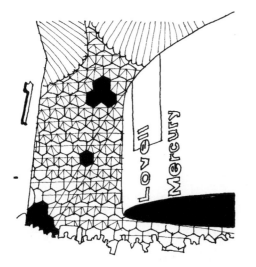

Figure 4.15 *Fuller and Sadao Inc., US Pavilion Expo '67, Montreal. From* Visual History of Twentieth Century Architecture, *Sharp, D., Heinemann, p. 280.*

tial freedom that framed structures offered architects in generating new plan types. Indeed, Le Corbusier's 'Five Points of the New Architecture' and most particularly his concept of the 'open' plan were dependent upon the minimal structural intrusion on plan that a framed structural type offered (**Figure 4.16**); rather than the intrusive and therefore restrictive 'footprint' of loadbearing walls (**Figure 4.17**), the minimal repetitive footprint of a column within a structural grid seemed to offer a new vocabulary of space enclosure. Moreover, by wilfully avoiding the columns, non-loadbearing partitions could weave on plan between them without challenging the primacy of the structural system (**Figure 4.18**).

seem to offer bewildering choices for the architect, the range of tectonic types (like plan types) is limited. For example, will the programme best be served by an 'ad-hoc' application of a traditional load-bearing masonry and timber type, or should advanced building technology be explored with its very different formal consequences? Which tectonic type will best 'fit' the plan type and parti (or diagram) for the building currently being explored?

Plan and structure

At this stage in the exploration it is worth considering how plan and structure interact. The modernists were quick to recognise the poten-

Figure 4.16 *Column and slab structure facilitating 'open plan'.*

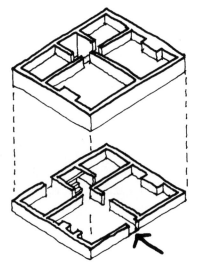

Figure 4.17   *Traditional house plan.*

Grid

But the repetitive grid of a structural frame also offers an ordering device to the architect as the building's diagram is developed so that plan and structure interact (**Figure 4.19**). Moreover, such a system of repetitive frames or 'bays' provides a primary order in which a secondary order of sub-systems may operate (**Figure 4.20**), and this potential for flexibility can allow the designer to 'add' or 'subtract' spaces from the primary structure without diluting its clarity. Lubetkin used this device to good effect at a house in Bognor Regis, Sussex, 1934 (**Figure 4.21**), and at Six Pillars, Dulwich, London, 1935 (**Figure 4.22**), where additive and subtractive spaces are used to mark entrances, to provide open terraces or projecting balconies, or are used

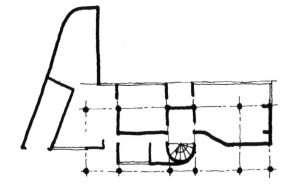

Figure 4.18   *Harding and Tecton, 'Six Pillars', Dulwich, London, 1934. Ground floor.*

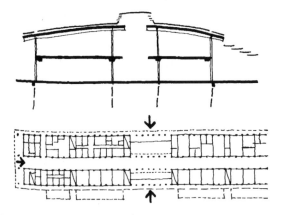

Figure 4.19   *Sir Norman Foster and Partners, School, Fréjus, France, 1995. From* Architectural Review *5/95, p. 64.*

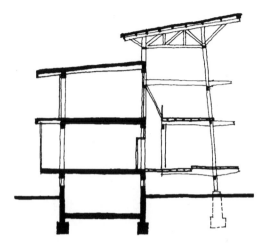

Figure 4.20 *Steidle and Partner, University Building, Ulm, Germany, 1992. Section.* Architectural Review 11/92, *p. 34.*

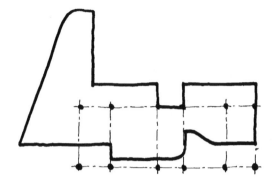

Figure 4.22 *Harding and Tecton, 'Six Pillars' Dulwich, London, 1934. Ground floor.*

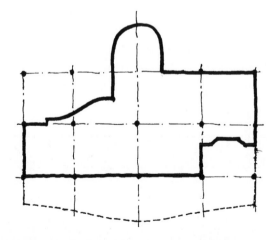

Figure 4.21 *Lubetkin and Tecton, House at Bognor Regis, Sussex, 1934. Ground floor.*

merely to fill left-over space in an irregular site between the boundary and a primary orthogonal structural grid.

Plane

But modernists also employed traditional structural types in pursuit of new attitudes towards space enclosure and form-making, exploring the potential of masonry walls as planes which loosely defined spaces rather than enclosing them as in a traditional cellular plan. Moreover, timber was used to create dramatic cantilevered roof planes in pursuit of a planar architecture which, whilst employing traditional materials and building techniques, owed nothing to tradition. And just as the repetitive structural grid had provided an ordering device to interact with the plan, so architects devised plan forms which were generated from a different kind of order; the disposition of wall and roof planes which itself reflected the limitations of a traditional building technology.

Mies van der Rohe's design for a Brick Country House of 1924 explored the potential of interrelated brickwork planes in liberating the plan (**Figure 4.23**) much in the manner of De Stijl attitudes towards space enclosure (**Figure 4.24**) whose origins could be traced back to Frank Lloyd Wright's 'prairie houses'; these had enjoyed an immense following in the Low Countries before and during the First World War following publication of the 'Wasmuth' volumes, a lavish production of Wright's *oeuvre* (Holland had remained neutral during that cataclysmic event and was able to develop its artistic movements unhindered by neighbouring hostilities). Wright developed these explorations still further in the celebrated 'Usonian' houses of the 1930s and 1940s

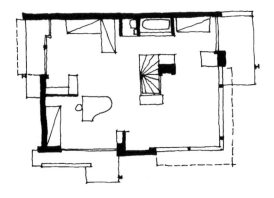

Figure 4.24 *Gerrit Rietveld, Schröder House, Utrecht, 1924. From* De Stijl,, *Overy, P., Studio Vista, p. 120.*

where a rationalised timber technology was associated with a masonry core to achieve a total correspondence between form-making, space enclosure and tectonics (**Figures 4.25, 4.26**).

James Stirling's design in 1955 for CIAM Rural Housing (**Figure 4.27**) also demonstrates how simply-ordered traditional building elements can generate a whole organisation in plan and section as well as being the major determinants of the building's formal outcome. Similarly, the work of Edward Cullinan and Peter Aldington has its roots in this tectonic tradition (**Figures 4.28, 4.29**) where a discipline of building technique has provided the principal clues for the 'diagram' and the functional plan. This attitude towards using technique as a springboard for the process of design has produced in its wake a

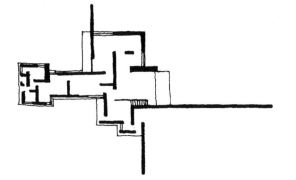

Figure 4.23 *Mies van der Rohe, Brick house, plan, 1923. From* Design in Architecture, *Broadbent, G., Wiley.*

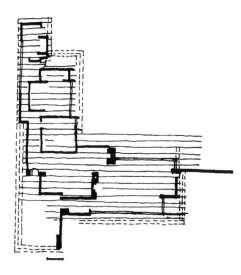

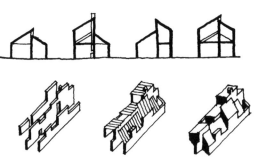

Figure 4.27 *James Stirling, Rural housing project, CIAM, 1955. From* The New Brutalism, *Banham, R., Architectural Press, p. 79.*

Figure 4.25 *Frank Lloyd Wright, Jacobs House, Wisconsin, 1937.*

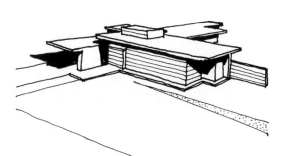

Figure 4.26 *Frank Lloyd Wright, Jacobs House, Wisconsin, 1937.*

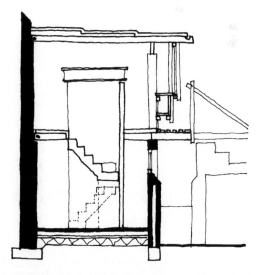

Figure 4.28 *Edward Cullinan, House, London, 1963. Section. From* Edward Cullinan Architects, *RIBA, p. 19.*

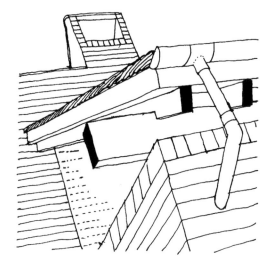

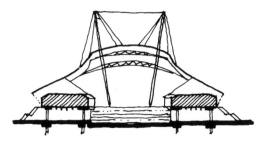

Figure 4.30 *Michael Hopkins, Inland Revenue Amenity Building, Nottingham, 1995. Section. From* Architectural Review *5/95, p. 40.*

Figure 4.29 *Aldington, Craig, Collinge. Housing, Bledlow, Bucks, 1977.*

powerful pragmatic tradition within the pluralist ambit of recent British architecture.

Just as most buildings juxtapose a range of formal framed, planar or plastic elements, so do they embody contrasting tectonic types. This may well be a response to a programme demanding a range of accommodation, the cellular elements of which could be served by a traditional structure of load-bearing masonry, but where other parts of the building demanding uncluttered spaces will require the technology of large spans.

Architects have seized upon the potential for form-making that such juxtapositions offer (**Figure 4.30**), but they also raise a question of structural hierarchies, where one structural form remains dominant over sub-systems which provide a secondary or even tertiary order.

Expression

Having arrived at an appropriate structure, or set of structural systems, be they framed, planar or plastic which will allow the 'diagram' to develop and mature, the designer is faced with the whole question of structural expression and how this interacts with the 'skin' of the building. Should the external membrane oversail and obscure a structural frame, should it infill and therefore express the frame, or should the frame be revealed as a free-standing element proud of the external cladding or 'skin' (**Figures 4.31–4.33**)?

Moreover, if load-bearing masonry structure is adopted, should the building in its external expression articulate a clear distinction between what is load-bearing and what is

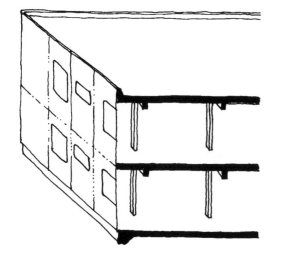

Figure 4.31   *Cladding 'oversailing' structure.*

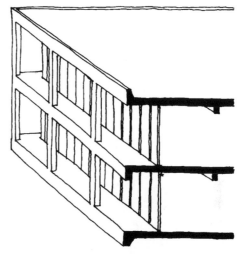

Figure 4.33   *Cladding recessed behind structure.*

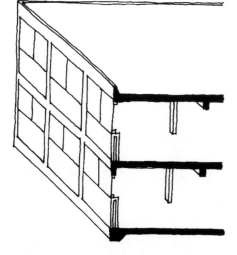

Figure 4.32   *Cladding 'flush' with structure.*

merely non-load-bearing infill. Therefore within this complex design process, attitudes towards choice of structure and its expression established at an early stage, inevitably have a profound effect upon a formal outcome.

HOW IS IT MADE?

Tectonic display

Having established what the 'carcass' or bare bones of the structure will be, the designer will give further thought to how these 'blocks', 'sticks' or 'membranes' will be assembled and joined together. As we shall see in the next chapter, this process in itself allows the designer plenty of scope for architectural expression, for just as architects of the functionalist school decreed that the nature of the 'carcass' should receive attention as an expressive element, so did they tend towards the view that the nature of materials making up the building's envelope, and more particularly, the manner of their assembly, should also contribute to 'reading' the building.

To the modernist there was something inherently satisfying about a building which was so explicit about its structure, its materials and its assembly and construction that it is not surprising that the pioneers of modernism looked to the work of contemporaneous structural, mechanical or nautical engineers and its naked expression of materials and assembly, for an acceptable *modus operandi* (**Figures 4.34–4.36**). But the pluralist world of so-called post-modernism in which we now find ourselves allows for alternative forms of architectural expression where other pressures, be they cultural or contextual, may well override

Figure 4.35 *1903 Renault.*

any perceived need to make an explicit display of structure, or constructional method.

The envelope

The majority of our constructional concerns relate to the design of the building's external envelope; the walls and roof membranes and how these are pierced for lighting or access. Decisions about the nature of this external

Figure 4.34 *Robert Stephenson, Britannia Bridge, Menai Strait, 1850. From* Architecture of the Nineteenth and Twentieth Century, *Hitchock, Penguin.*

Figure 4.36 *The Flandre. From* Towards a New Architecture, *Architectural Press, p. 81.*

'skin' to the building will not only interact with other major decisions as the design develops, but will also determine to a large extent how the building will look.

The roof

Take the roof for example; will it be flat or pitched, and in either case will it project beyond the wall plane to afford some protection from the weather or will it be arrested behind a parapet wall? Should the roof be considered as a lightweight 'umbrella' structurally and visually separate from the principal structural idea (**Figure 4.37**), or does that idea also produce the roof envelope merely by the application of a waterproof membrane (**Figure 4.38**)? These fundamental questions of whether the roof is a lightweight or a heavyweight envelope (with a considerable thermal mass) have real consequences regarding the building's appearance but also its performance.

Flat roof technology has developed so that insulation is positioned at the 'cold' side of any heavyweight roof, allowing the structural thermal mass to work in favour of the building's thermal performance. Not surprisingly, the flat roof (or a roof with minimum falls to points of rainwater collection) will be considered as a continuous impervious skin whether that skin is applied to a heavyweight structure or to a lightweight roof 'deck'. But as to pitched roofs, decisions regarding a lightweight impermeable and continuous membrane as opposed to a heavy roof of traditional provenance formed from individual tiles or slates which are by their nature permeable, will again

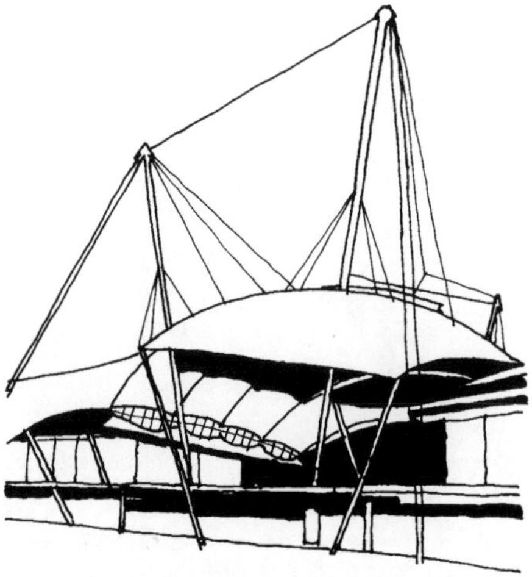

Figure 4.37 *Michael Hopkins, Inland Revenue Amenity Building, Nottingham, 1995. Section. From* Architectural Review 5/95, *p. 46.*

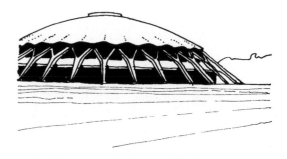

Figure 4.38 *P. L. Nervi, Palace of Sport, Rome, 1957. From* Visual History of the Twentieth Century Architecture, *Sharp, D., p. 213.*

have a profound effect upon the building's appearance. Moreover, the particular materials employed in the latter case will determine the limit of inclination or pitch for the roof plane; the larger the tile or slate, the lower the pitch which may be effected. Clearly such constraints also contribute to the visual outcome of any roof (**Figures 4.39, 4.40**).

Another strategic element of roof design is how rainwater is to be collected. It is important to realise how such an apparently mundane and banal proposition as rainwater collection can have a profound effect upon how a building looks. Many architects have seized upon expressive devices at the roof's edge to collect water from the roof membrane and then discharge it (**Figures 4.41, 4.42**); exaggerated

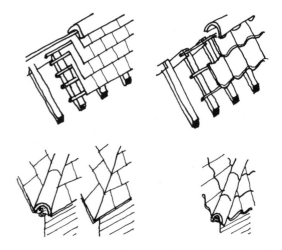

Figure 4.40 *Traditional heavy slate and pantile roofs.*

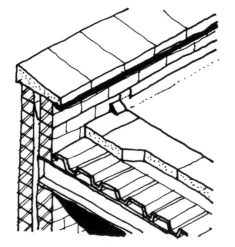

Figure 4.39 *Lightweight roof 'deck'.*

Figure 4.41 *Le Corbusier, Chapel, Ronchamp, France, 1955.*

Figure 4.42 *Ralph Erskine, Clare Hall, Cambridge, 1968. Rainwater chute.*

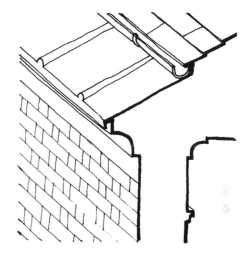

Figure 4.43 *Donald MacMorran, Social Science Building, Nottingham University, 1957. Eaves detail.*

projecting eaves have rendered such expression even more explicit (**Figure 4.42**). In contradistinction to this approach, some architects have chosen to conceal gutters and downpipes (with obvious consequences for future maintenance) within the building fabric. Where a pitched roof is employed, this may result in a minimal roof surface of projecting eaves beyond the building's edge shedding water to the ground without recourse to any system of collection (**Figure 4.43**). In any event it is important to understand the visual consequences of such decision-making.

The façade

Like the roof, the wall membrane is an 'environmental filter' which contributes to the buil-

ding's performance and decisions regarding lightweight versus heavyweight, or permeable versus impermeable which applied to the roof likewise need to be considered. But in the case of walls these decisions assume a greater degree of complexity for, much more than roofs, walls tend to be punctuated by openings to provide access, daylighting, views out, or ventilation, all of which have to be accommodated within the strategy for construction.

Should traditional loadbearing structure be employed, then the wall membrane will be 'heavy' and most likely permeable. Moreover, openings are likely to be formed within this heavy membrane by simple lintels which suggests a directly expressive 'hole-in-the-wall' architecture (**Figure 4.44**). By con-

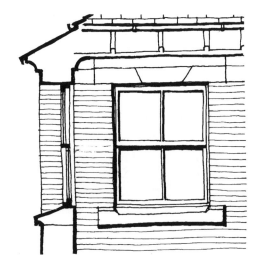

Figure 4.44 *Donald MacMorran, Social Science Building, Nottingham University, 1957. Window detail.*

and in the process provide the principal generator of architectural expression, openings appearing in the monolithic screen as and when required. Alternatively, the screen may be considered as repetitive panels which may oversail the structure but junctions between panels will conform to the structural grid; in such a situation the design of panels to allow for a range of openings determines the architectural expression (**Figure 4.45**). Moreover, it is possible to express the structural frame within both light and heavy envelopes; at its most basic, the frame remains proud of the cladding (**Figure 4.46**) or is simply infilled (**Figure 4.47**).

It is not our purpose here to provide a manual of building construction techniques but rather

trast, a structural frame opens up a whole range of alternatives for considering the nature of the external wall. At one level, a non-structural traditional heavy envelope may conceal structural columns, beams and floor slabs and may employ a traditional 'hole-in-the-wall' expression thereby flouting the modernist orthodoxy for structural 'honesty' (this has become much less of a 'sacred cow' since the emergence of a post-modern pluralism).

But just as a repetitive framed structure has liberated the plan so has it liberated the façade. Architects are now faced with a range of devices to express 'wall' which may or may not express the primary structure. At one level a lightweight impervious 'rainscreen' may oversail the frame

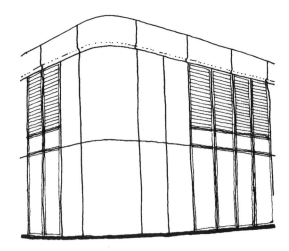

Figure 4.45 *Nicholas Grimshaw and Partners, Factory, Bath, England, 1976.*

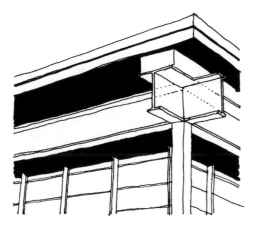

Figure 4.46 *Roche, Dinkeloo, Factory, Darlington, 1964.*

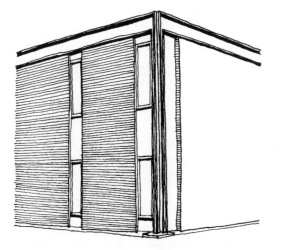

Figure 4.47 *James Cubitt and Partners with Eero Saarinen, Factory, Darlington, 1964.*

to articulate a range of attitudes and options open to the designer. Clearly the nature of the membrane is determined by the nature of the materials which it comprises, whether heavy or light, permeable or impermeable, monolithic or comprising a variety of distinct components. However, most of our constructional concerns not unnaturally surround the whole question of joining one element to another. At a fundamental level, how is the wall connected to the roof and how does the wall meet the floor? And how does a cladding membrane join the structure? How do we achieve a satisfactory junction between solid and void, opaque and transparent elements within the building's 'skin'?

The outcome of all of these questions will have a powerful effect upon the building's appearance and therefore upon how we 'read' the building. We have already discussed how a clear 'diagram' involving the functional plan and structural expression allows us to 'read' and assimilate a building's organisation. This notion may be further extended to construction so that the building is also 'read' at a detailed level where secondary and tertiary elements which make up the building add to an understanding of and are consistent with the primary design decisions surrounding the diagram or *parti*.

Consequently, design seen in this context is a reiterative process where themes are introduced and repeated throughout the building, externally and internally; materials and constructional techniques employed within the building's external fabric may be applied internally in pursuit of 'thematic' consistency.

WILL IT BE COMFORTABLE?

Just as a designer's attitudes towards structure and how that structure is clad may profoundly affect the form-making process, so may our stance regarding environmental comfort have a powerful bearing upon that formal outcome. And just as architects harnessed new technologies of structure and construction to liberate the plan, so did an artificially controlled internal environment remove traditional planning limitations; the option now existed for creating deep-planned buildings freed from the organisational constraints of natural ventilation and lighting.

This brings us yet again to the notion of 'type' and its central position in the design process for not only, as previously discussed, can 'type' inform our attitudes towards 'plan' and 'structure', but it can also determine how the various criteria for environmental comfort are to be met.

Active v passive

Therefore, the designer may decide that comfort will be achieved totally by artificial means where heating, ventilation and lighting standards are met by the installation of sophisticated mechanical and electrical plant. This may be considered to be one 'type' where the internal environment is subjected entirely to artificial control. At the other extreme, the designer may wish to harness the building's inherent characteristics in a passive way to control levels of comfort.

Historically, such were the constraints of natural ventilation and lighting, that designers were forced into the orthodoxy of a narrow plan for efficient cross-ventilation from opening windows, and a generous floor-ceiling height to maximise levels of natural lighting (**Figure 4.48**). By way of a bonus such buildings of heavy traditional construction also

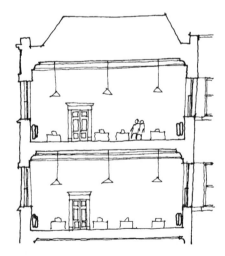

Figure 4.48 *Nineteenth-century office, typical section.*

offered considerable thermal mass for passive cooling in summer and heat retention in winter. But with the move during the mid-twentieth century towards a totally artificial environment, architects found themselves no longer constrained by a narrow plan typology and were free to explore the potential of deep plans. Therefore as these systems developed in their levels of sophistication, so the traditional role of the building fabric itself as an 'environmental filter' was displaced (**Figure 4.49**).

So just as framed and large-span structures developed during the nineteenth century modified a traditional correspondence between plan and structure, so did the development of

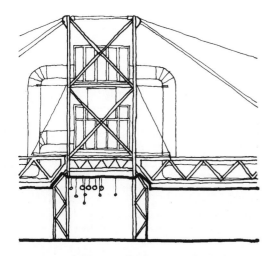

Figure 4.49   *Richard Rogers, Inmos Factory, Newport, Wales, 1982. From* Richard Rogers Architectural Monographs, *Academy, p. 65.*

mechanical servicing within buildings during the twentieth century replace the inherent environmental capability of traditional building forms. And moreover, just as progressive architects seized upon new structural forms for fresh architectural expression in the early twentieth century, so did the next generation exploit the expressive quality of tubes, ducts and plant associated with mechanical servicing.

Clearly, the selection by the designer of an 'environmental' type has consequences upon the development and outcome of the design as profound as considerations of type when applied to 'structure' and 'plan'. All such types must be considered simultaneously and are inherently interactive. Therefore at one extreme we arrive at a type entirely dependent upon the mechanical control of heating, cooling and ventilation for thermal comfort and upon permanent artificial lighting. At the other, a type emerges which embraces purely passive measures in achieving acceptable levels of comfort, not only harnessing the building fabric to achieve natural ventilation and lighting, but also potentially using the building as a collector of available solar and wind energy; in extreme cases such buildings may exceed in energy generation their energy consumption.

But most environmental types fall between these two extremes and just as architects initially embraced an emergent technology of mechanical ventilation to assist an inherently passive traditional system, so do most types emerge as hybrid systems.

The orthodoxy of an artificial environment served by mechanical means of high energy consumption was to undergo a fundamental revision largely on account of the so-called 'energy crisis' of the 1970s. Architects reconsidered and reinterpreted traditional passive methods of environmental control which did not rely upon profligate levels of energy consumption and this fundamental shift in attitude was applied to a range of building types to produce a new orthodoxy for the latter part of the twentieth century. As already indicated, such changing attitudes were profoundly to affect the formal outcome of established building types; the reversion to 'narrow' plans (**Figure 4.50**), the development of the enclosed 'atrium' form (**Figure 4.51**), and such devices as 'thermal chimneys' (**Figure 4.52**) were all developed as part of this passive revival, and architects were quick to recognise their potential for form-making.

Architectural expression

The outcome of such concerns for energy consumption has been a profound modification of established *partis* for a range of building types as diverse as offices, hospitals, health centres, housing and schools. Presciently pre-dating the energy crisis by several years, St. George's School, Wallasey, Cheshire, by E.

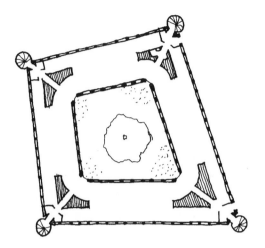

Figure 4.50 *Michael Hopkins and Partners, Inland Revenue Offices, Nottingham, 1995. Ground floor plan. From* Architectural Review *5/95, p. 34.*

A. Morgan, 1961, was a pioneering example of harnessing solar energy. Central to the environmental functioning of the building was the 'solar wall' whose height and length to a large extent predetermined the form and orientation of the building. As a heat source

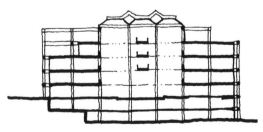

Figure 4.51 *Arup Associates, Office, Basingstoke, England, 1985. From* The Environmental Tradition, *Hawkes, D., Spon, p. 156.*

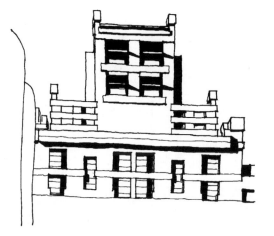

Figure 4.52 *Peake Short and Partners, Brewery, Malta, Thermal chimney, 1901.*

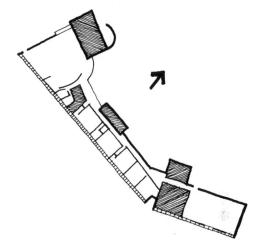

Figure 4.53 *Emslie Morgan, Wallasey School, 1961.* From The Environmental Tradition, *Hawkes, D., Spon, p. 122.*

this was supplemented by electric light fittings and the building's occupants, an early example of heat recovery. But the plan type, a linear single bank of teaching spaces, south facing and with corridor access and lavatory accommodation on the north side, is entirely subservient to the functioning of the solar wall (**Figure 4.53**). Moreover, the section incorporates a steep monopitched roof to accommodate the tall solar wall, and offering much reduced headroom to a heavily insulated and minimally fenestrated north elevation (**Figure 4.54**). Therefore the whole 'diagram' for the building and its formal outcome departed fundamentally from an established 'linked pavilion' or 'courtyard' type for school building in favour of a clear 'linear' organisa-

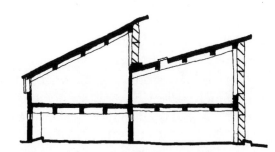

Figure 4.54 *Emslie Morgan, Wallasey School, 1961.* From The Environmental Tradition, *Hawkes, D., Spon, p. 120.*

tion as a direct result of a radical environmental strategy.

At the Inland Revenue offices, Nottingham, 1995, Michael Hopkins demonstrated how considerations of heating, cooling and lighting were major factors in generating a plan form well-removed from a prevailing deep-plan orthodoxy. In the event, a medium-rise courtyard type prevailed as a direct consequence of this strategy, but also suggesting an appropriate model for extending an existing 'grain' of the city onto redundant inner-city sites. At the onset of the design process it was decided to avoid air conditioning, but to harness ambient energy and natural lighting as much as possible. The outcome is a narrow plan which gives views through (opening) windows to internal courtyards or to external public 'boulevards'. Moreover, masonry piers supporting exposed precast concrete floor slabs provide substantial thermal mass to maintain an equable internal environment (**Figure 4.55**). The expression of these massive piers and the barrel-vaulted floor slabs which they support help us to 'read' the building but also provide a repetitive rhythm and 'scale' to the elevations. Moreover, the light shelves which reflect daylight deep into the plan and the low-level louvres which prevent the penetration of winter sun are also used to impart an intensity to the scale of the building. Cylindrical thermal chimneys extract air from the offices, accommodate the stairs, and offer

Figure 4.55 Michael Hopkins and Partners, Inland Revenue Offices, Nottingham, 1995. From Architectural Review 5/95, p. 37.

an external 'marker' to the points of entry (**Figure 4.56**). The result is a satisfying correspondence of plan type, structural and environmental types, formal outcome and detailed architectural expression.

WILL IT BE GREEN?

So far we have established how specific tectonic decisions regarding structure, construction, or environmental performance may affect the formal outcome of our building design, but what of the much broader issue of sustainabil-

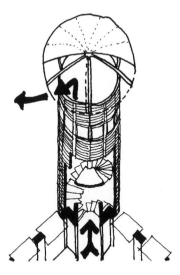

Figure 4.56 *Sir Michael Hopkins and Partners, Inland Revenue Offices, Nottingham, 1995. Thermal chimney. From* Architectural Review 5/95, p. 35.

ity and its potential for influencing architectural form?

Attitudes towards achieving a sustainable environment gathered considerable momentum during the latter quarter of the twentieth century. Consequently, architects practising in this century now view sustainability as a central plank of their professional skills, and a necessary addition to those traditions already aggregated.

But what do we mean by sustainability? At its broadest, a sustainable environment will be healthy for its inhabitants, will be economic during its life span, and will be capable of adapting to society's changing needs. Many

buildings throughout history have, indeed, satisfied these criteria and may be deemed sustainable, but conversely, many (particularly from the twentieth century) have not. Instead they have met with premature obsolescence and, in many cases, demolition.

But for the architect, much of sustainability surrounds the minimising of fossil fuel consumption with an attendant reduction of greenhouse gas emission (of which carbon dioxide represents the main component), which contributes to global warming. The orthodoxy of deep-plan, mechanically air-conditioned buildings which relied on high levels of permanent artificial lighting, and often used materials of high embodied energy (**Figure 4.57**), has been replaced by buildings designed for natural lighting and ventilation, which harness alternative forms of energy such as solar or wind power (**Figure 4.58**). This suggests a design regime where climate and site can fundamentally influence primary design decisions. Moreover, such buildings will conserve energy and will be constructed of re-usable materials with minimal environ-

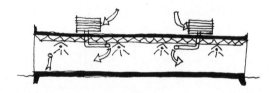

Figure 4.57 *Deep-plan orthodoxy.*

Figure 4.58 'Sustainable' orthodoxy.

mental impact in their manufacture and transport to the site.

In the pursuit of sustainable architecture, this suggests a further 'sub-set' of design principles to add to those discussed elsewhere: harnessing climate and natural energy sources; selecting re-cyclable materials of low embodied energy; and energy conservation. Arguably, these principles are long established in architectural history, and have only recently been rediscovered to represent the architectural aspirations of the twenty-first century, but it is their interaction which promises a new 'holistic' architecture with genuine sustainable credentials and fresh opportunities for formal invention.

Climate and natural energy

Harnessing the climate to improve human comfort is nothing new; the Greeks and Romans well recognised the benefits of designing dwellings whose principal rooms faced south to improve thermal comfort. But in some climates, designers are met with the problem of cooling spaces to improve comfort, and here, similarly, we can look to tradition. High-density Middle Eastern courtyard housing used shade and a water fountain to cool air within the courtyard, which was then exhausted via wind towers to assist cooling of the habitable rooms (**Figure 4.59**). Window openings were kept to a minimum to restrict solar gain. By contrast, the traditional Malay house moderated a tropical climate by using a framed structure of low thermal mass with overhanging eaves to a pitched roof, which offered shading from the sun but also protection from monsoon rains. Wall openings at roof level provided cross ventilation to assist cooling (**Figure 4.60**).

But how have contemporary designers used climate as a source of renewable energy to

Figure 4.59 Middle East courtyard house.

Figure 4.60 *Malay house-on-stilts.*

heat, light, and cool buildings and to improve comfort? Most techniques involve solar energy used actively and passively, or wind power.

Passive solar energy

Because passive systems of recovering solar energy are readily accessible, and after twenty years' development have reached a sophisticated level, they are the most prevalent. At a fundamental level, passive solar design depends upon: (a) principal façades facing south-east to south-west; (b) the site's orientation and gradient; (c) avoiding overshadowing on site from existing obstructions; and (d) avoiding overshadowing from obstructions beyond the site boundary. Passive systems embrace simple direct gain (of solar energy), indirect gain, or a combination of both.

Direct gain, as its name implies, depends upon a majority of the building's fenestration facing south-east—south west (for the northern

hemisphere) so that solar radiation enters the building directly. Ideally, such fenestration should relate to principal spaces, relegating purely service areas to north-facing façades. The high thermal mass of floor slabs in direct contact with solar radiation can be used as a thermal 'store' to moderate internal temperature fluctuations; in domestic situations, the warmed floor slab will release its stored heat during the evening when occupancy is likely to be at its highest. At night, the detailed design of fenestration (preferably triple-glazed with low-emissivity glass) can assist this heat retention by including internal insulated blinds; daytime overheating in summer can be reduced by incorporating external shading devices (blinds or louvres), or simply by extending the canopy of roof eaves. Analysis of existing direct gain systems in domestic applications suggests that the dwelling depth should be limited to 12 m and that solar glazing should be no more than 35 per cent of the room's floor area. For optimal solar collection in the UK, roof pitch should be at 30° to 40° with solar façades at 60° to 70° from the horizontal (**Figure 4.61**).

Indirect gain depends upon an 'interface' of high thermal mass located between the sun and habitable spaces, so that solar energy is transferred indirectly to the interior. The Trombe wall is the most common 'indirect gain' device and employs a 300 mm thermal storage wall located between an outer skin of glazing and habitable space. Its area should

Figure 4.61 *Direct solar gain.*

Figure 4.62 *Trombe wall.*

not exceed 20 per cent of the area which it heats. Just as the floor slab in direct gain systems releases its stored heat slowly, so the Trombe wall allows its stored heat to be transmitted to the interior at a rate depending upon its thickness. The outer skin of glazing provides a rain screen but also contributes to heat retention through an inherent 'greenhouse' effect. The Trombe's efficiency is enhanced by incorporating vents at its base and head, which connect the glazed void to the habitable space; by convection, air from the room is tempered and re-circulated (**Figure 4.62**).

The familiar conservatory or 'sunspace' embraces both direct and indirect solar gain and provides, economically, a flexible exten-

sion to habitable space. Thermal isolation will reduce heat loss from an adjacent room in winter and will control heat gain in summer. Vents will allow for a moderating air flow between the conservatory and its adjoining space (**Figure 4.63**).

Active solar energy

There are two types of active solar systems; those which directly use the sun's rays (as in a flat plate collector) and those which convert solar energy into another power source (as in photovoltaic cells). Both collectors are mounted on south-facing roofs at optimum pitch (30° to 40°).

Figure 4.63 *Attached 'sunspace'.*

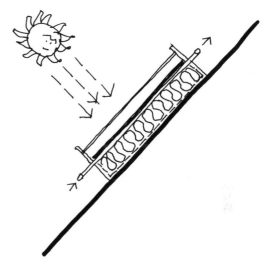

Figure 4.64 *Flat plate solar collector.*

The flat plate collector is essentially a water-filled calorifier behind an absorber plate, which transfers solar heat to another medium. In the UK, it is generally used for domestic hot water systems, where roof-mounted collectors heat water storage tanks within the roofspace (**Figure 4.64**).

Photovoltaic (PV) cells convert solar energy into electrical power which is then harnessed within the building for space heating, cooling, mechanical ventilation, or lighting. They embody two layers of semi-conducting material which, when exposed to sunlight, generate electrical power. They are normally incorporated within roof or wall cladding systems, and in some installations offer sun shading.

Embodied energy and recycling

The 'embodied' energy of materials within a building is complex, and relates to how such materials can be recycled after the building's 'first use', as well as to the energy used in their manufacture and transport to the site. Moreover, embodied energy is small (approximately 10 per cent) when compared with that consumed during a building's useful life.

The English Arts and Crafts architects, notably Ernest Gimson (**Figure 4.65**) and Edward Prior, sourced their building materials as near

Figure 4.65 *Ernest Gimson: Stoneywell Cottage, Leics.*

to the site as possible. This both satisfied their ideological concerns and their regard for utility, but well pre-dated the widespread use of lightweight building materials sourced internationally. Therefore in the interests of sustainability, heavyweight materials such as masonry and aggregates for making concrete, should be sourced locally, but for most lightweight materials, the embodied energy in transporting them to the site is far outstripped by that consumed during manufacture, suggesting that local sourcing is less critical.

There are two categories of recycling; one re-uses the salvaged building materials and components 'as found' in a new building, whilst the other manufactures new components from 'scrap' material. The embodied energy of the latter is much greater.

On a larger scale, some buildings offer an infinite capacity for re-use, whilst others, because of an inherent inflexibility in their organisation and method of construction, face demolition after the expiry of their 'first life'.

Energy conservation

Whilst buildings which are heavily insulated and air-tight will conserve energy, sensible design decisions at a strategic stage are nevertheless crucial in this pursuit. For example, north-facing fenestration should be minimal, or *in extremis*, avoided altogether. This simple case exposes the interactive nature of sustainable design, for high levels of insulation will not produce 'green' architecture should embodied energy, or working with a prevailing climate, be disregarded.

Nevertheless, high insulation represents an economic way of dramatically reducing a building's energy requirement and therefore its consumption of fossil-based fuels. A building's thermal performance can easily be measured, and this quantitative component of sustainable design has led to 'superinsulated' buildings, particularly in the domestic sector, where the benefits of 300 mm thick wall insulation and 500 mm thick roof insulation can be readily calculated (**Figure 4.66**). Locating such insu-

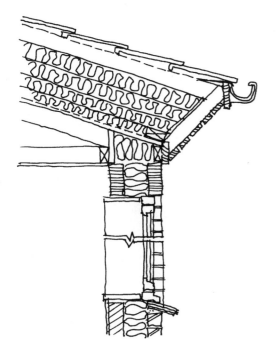

Figure 4.66 *Superinsulation: Robert and Brenda Vale, Woodhouse Medical Centre, Sheffield.*

lation on the 'cold' side of heavyweight walls, floors, and roofs will allow the thermal mass of these elements to moderate the internal environment by heat retention in winter and by passive cooling in summer. Vapour barriers should be located at the 'warm' side of insulation; openings in the building's fabric and junctions between constructional elements should be airtight.

So what effect has sustainability had upon architectural form? Certainly, architects have extended their range of architectural expres-

sion both at strategic and tactical levels. The response to climate is obvious in a new orthodoxy of heavily-glazed south elevations with shading devices (**Figure 4.67**) and attendant minimally-glazed north elevations on a narrow plan, with direct visual consequences. Moreover, devices such as atria and thermal chimneys (**Figure 4.68**) have been displayed by architects as expressive elements to describe their building's 'green' credentials.

In extreme cases, such as Hockerton housing in Nottinghamshire, UK, by Robert and Brenda Vale (**Figure 4.67**), traditional modes of architectural expression have been virtually subsumed by a need to satisfy the 'green' agenda. Even though a menu of traditional materials has been employed, they construct south-facing sunspaces, earth sheltering to north and east elevations, and turf-covered roofs, to establish a fresh and distinctive architectural expression for domestic buildings.

Figure 4.67 *Passive solar housing: Robert and Brenda Vale, Hockerton Housing, UK.*

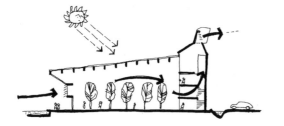

Figure 4.68 *Atrium diagram: Michael Hopkins, Jubilee campus, Nottingham University, UK.*

On a larger scale, Michael Hopkins employed the whole gamut of sustainable devices at Jubilee Campus, Nottingham University, UK (**Figure 4.68**). Atria with glazed roofs incorporating PV cells, light shelves, louvred shading devices, thermal chimneys, and grass roofs, are all overtly displayed as powerful elements within a new architectural expression, and, in the event, extend that modernist concern for tectonic display to mainstream contemporary architecture.

5 HOW WILL IT LOOK?

Throughout history, but particularly during the twentieth century, architects have been seduced by powerful visual images which have been reinterpreted (or misapplied) in building types quite divorced in function and scale from the seminal work which provided the image in the first place. Therefore, the visual imagery of Le Corbusier's Villa Savoye (**Figure 5.1**), a weekend house in Poissy for a wealthy bourgeois Parisian family, has been freely applied to such diverse buildings as a scientific research establishment (**Figure 5.2**) or a parish church (**Figure 5.3**). Moreover, by way of emphasising the inherent longevity of such images, these reinterpretations post-date the original by as much as four decades.

It has already been suggested that very early in the design process, architects have in their mind's eye some notion, however tentative, of how their building will look, and as we have already seen, most decisions made by the architect towards prosecuting a building design have profound visual consequences.

This has been demonstrated at a primary level of arriving at appropriate 'types' for plan, structure and environmental strategy, for example. But what of secondary or tertiary decisions regarding the building's 'skin'?

EXPRESSION v SUPPRESSION

However, be it for symbolic or contextual reasons, or even to satisfy the designer's stylistic predilections, expression of the external skin of the building may override any considerations for plan, structure and construction. *In extremis* such attitudes lead us to historical revivalism where the 'façade' literally disguises all potential for tectonic display (**Figure 5.4**); whilst this may be one intriguing manifestation of a pluralist world, nevertheless, because of an obsession with limited stylistic concerns, such a course inevitably leads to an architectural cul de sac.

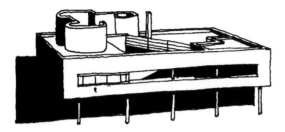

Figure 5.1 *Le Corbusier, Villa Savoye, Poissy, 1931. From student model, University of Nottingham.*

Figure 5.3 *Derek Walker, Chief Architect, Milton Keynes Development Corporation, Parish Church, Milton Keynes, 1974.*

It was Lubetkin who remarked that one of the most difficult tasks facing the architect was giving a building 'a hat and a pair of boots'. In the event he followed the Corbusian example of allowing the building to 'hover' over the site on free-standing columns, thereby offering a transitional void between the building and the site; at roof level, a carefully organised repetitive façade was terminated by an eruption of plastic formal incident which effectively finished off the building with a silhouette akin to abstract sculpture (**Figure 5.5**). These devices

were initially established by Le Corbusier embodied within his 'five points' manifesto and were best exploited on multi-storey buildings, but even when faced with designing his own single-storey dwelling at Whipsnade, Bedfordshire, 1936, Lubetkin reinterpreted the Corbusian model by cantilevering the floor slab from its primary support so that the whole structure appeared to be visually

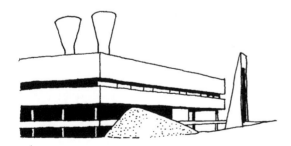

Figure 5.2 *Ryder and Yates, Gas Council Research Station, Killingworth, Northumberland, 1969.*

Figure 5.4 *Quinlan Terry, Library, Downing College, Cambridge, 1992.*

Figure 5.5 *Le Corbusier, Unité d'Habitation, Marseilles, 1952.*

ing a satisfactory transition between the building and the ground, and, indeed, for terminating the façade at roof level; such were the roles of the rusticated base and entablature respectively and architects have since reinterpreted these devices in various ways (**Figure 5.7**). Whilst various alternatives to the classical base or podium have been evolved as plinths firmly to wed the building to its site, it is the role of the roof in determining how a building looks which has most taxed architects' visual imaginations.

divorced from the site. At roof level, a curved wall within the plan was reiterated as a plastic screen addressing the surrounding landscape (**Figure 5.6**).

The classical language of architecture had offered a whole range of devices for establish-

Figure 5.6 *Berthold Lubetkin, House at Whipsnade, 1936. From* Berthold Lubetkin, *Allen, J., RIBA, p. 186.*

Figure 5.7 *T. C. Howitt, Portland Building, Nottingham University, 1957.*

ROOF

The first question to ask is whether the roof should assume a major visual role or whether it should remain obscured behind a parapet wall. The notion of 'parapet' generally suggests a heavy wall envelope with a flat roof concealed behind it, whereas the decision to use a pitched roof generates a range of possibilities not only regarding roof form (steep/shallow or dual/mono pitch, for example) but also regarding the nature of the membrane (heavy/light), and more particularly, how the roof and wall effect a satisfactory junction.

Just as a structural grid can assist in ordering a plan, so can a pitched roof give order to the building's final form by providing a dominant canopy to which all other formal interventions are secondary. Wright's prairie houses, with their low-pitched roofs and massively projecting eaves illustrate how a dominant roof can bring together and unify subservient visual incident (**Figure 5.8**). Furthermore, it is possible visually to enrich the roof by tectonic display; exposed rafters, trusses and how they connect with supporting walls and columns offer an endless range of visual incident for the designer to explore (**Figure 5.9**). Part of this overt display can involve rainwater collection from the roof; architects have exaggerated gutters, gargoyles, downpipes and water shutes to gain

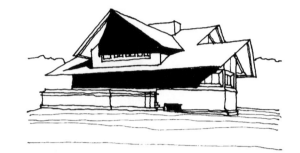

Figure 5.8 *Frank Lloyd Wright, Warren Hickox House, Kankalee, Illinois, 1900. From* Architecture of the Nineteenth and Twentieth Century, *Hitchock, Pelican, p. 376.*

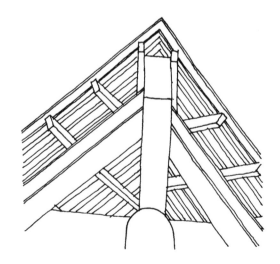

Figure 5.9 *David Thurlow, Eurocentre, Cambridge, 1985.*

maximum visual effect from the simply utilitarian (**Figure 5.10**).

And how will the roof turn a corner? Will the chosen eaves detail be repeated at every corner and re-entrant so that a 'hip' and a 'valley' respectively are the inevitable result (**Figure 5.11**), or will the corner reveal a 'gable' and a 'verge' (**Figure 5.12**)? Will the verge project beyond the wall plane to expose purlins and rafters (**Figure 5.13**), or will the verge be 'clipped' (**Figure 5.14**), or even concealed behind a parapet? Will such a change in roof treatment at a corner imply an elevational hierarchy and the inevitable consequences in 'reading' the building?

If the plan is deep or if internal circulation routes need daylight it will be necessary to

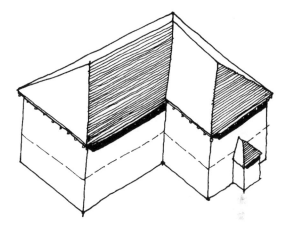

Figure 5.11   Hipped and valleyed roof.

penetrate the roof membrane with some form of roof light. Again, the form these rooflights take will have visual consequences both internally and externally. It is as well to group rooflights or make them a continuous extrusion so that they are of sufficient visual mass to 'read'

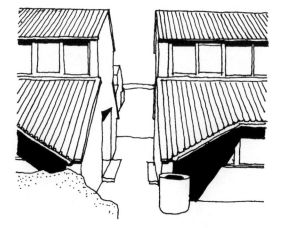

Figure 5.10   Edward Cullinan, Housing, Highgrove, London, 1972.

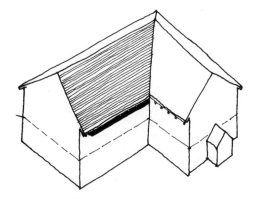

Figure 5.12   Gabled roof.

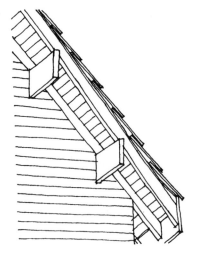

Figure 5.13 *Projecting verge.*

as part of a design strategy. It is possible to place a continuous rooflight at a roof's ridge simply within the roof plane, elevated (**Figure 5.15**), or projecting one roof plane beyond another to form 'dormers' (**Figure 5.16**). The latter solution has the benefit of offering reflected light off the ceiling plane.

We have already seen how the choice of wall membrane can profoundly affect a building's appearance; whether heavy or light, loadbearing or non-structural infill to a frame. But the wall must also accommodate openings for access, lighting, views out and ventilation as well as providing aesthetically satisfactory connections with roof, intermediate floors and the ground. The wall must also turn corners so that quoins and re-entrants are significant visual events rather than mere planning expedients.

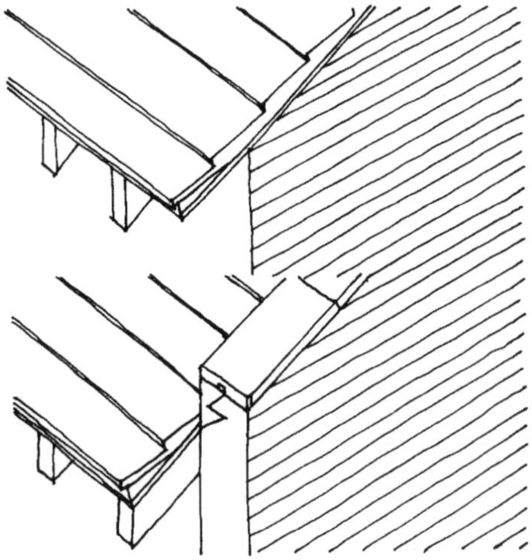

Figure 5.14 *Clipped/parapet verge.*

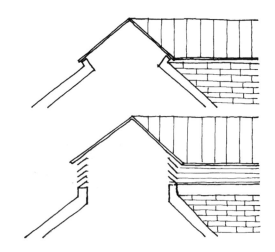

Figure 5.15 *Continuous rooflight.*

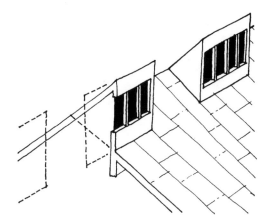

Figure 5.16 *Ridge 'dormer' window.*

OPENINGS

Planning the pattern of openings in an external wall has long exercised the designer's imagination; the classical language of architecture offered an ordering system of proportions for this task which Le Corbusier was to reinterpret as variously 'Regulating Lines', and 'Le Modulor'. These were evolved to ensure a building's order and harmony, including its elevational treatment.

Whilst the primary consideration when placing orifices within the wall must be the provision of light and access, areas of void within an elevation may have other purposes. For example, entrances have symbolic importance as thresholds and such openings must be fashioned with this in mind. Moreover, within a framed building a continuous clerestory window may effect by separation a visual transition between roof and wall (**Figure 5.17**); should the eaves project, this will also provide reflected light from the roof's external soffit, an effect heightened if the soffit projects over water. In a similar fashion vertical strips of glazing adjacent to a column can highlight the column, again assisting in the process of 'reading' a framed building (**Figure 5.18**).

ELEVATIONS

Indeed, as has already been indicated, our whole attitude towards structure, its expression

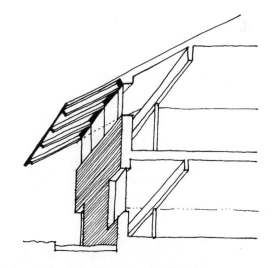

Figure 5.17 *Clerestory/roof/wall junction.*

Figure 5.18 *William Whitfield, Geography Building, Sheffield University, 1974.*

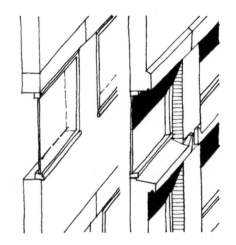

Figure 5.19 *Flush/recessed fenestration.*

or suppression, and how structure interacts with openings within the fabric, can profoundly influence the elevational outcome of buildings. Even within a simple loadbearing masonry wall there are several ways in which window openings may be fashioned and these are determined largely by relationships between the plane of the wall and the plane of the glass. It is possible for the glass to be flush with the external wall so that the elevation reads as a taut plane; this will give generous reveals and cills internally which will reflect light and help to minimise glare. Conversely, should the glass coincide with the internal wall face then deep external reveals will impart a robustness to the façade absent in the former example (**Figure 5.19**). Developing the eleva-

tion further, the designer may wish to express cills, lintels, light shelves and external shading devices further to articulate the façade and to provide visual intensity (**Figure 5.20**). Moreover the design of openings may indicate by differentiation, a hierarchy of spaces which they serve, again helping us to 'read' the building.

WALL MEMBRANES

The idea of 'layering' a series of planes to form the wall takes on further meaning when dealing with framed structures whose wall membranes have no structural function other than resisting wind loads. At one level, a structural frame may be totally obscured by a heavy

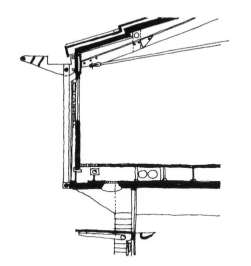

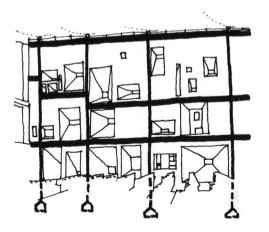

Figure 5.21 Le Corbusier, Chapel, Ronchamp, France, 1955. Location of columns and beams in wall.

Figure 5.20 Michael Hopkins and Partners, Inland Revenue Offices, Nottingham, 1995. From Architectural Review 5/95, p. 36.

cladding which looks as if it is loadbearing, suggesting that the designer has had other priorities in fashioning the elevational treatment than straightforward structural expression. This was certainly the case in the chapel at Ronchamp by Le Corbusier where massive rendered walls of rubble completely conceal a reinforced concrete frame which supports the shell-like roof. An apparently random fenestration pattern is ordered not only by the Modulor proportioning device, but also by the requirement to avoid the column positions buried within the wall (**Figure 5.21**).

Clearly, the location of the wall plane in relation to the column is the primary decision when designing the elevations of framed buildings. The wall may oversail the columns which then will be revealed internally, roof and floors cantilevering beyond them to connect with the cladding (**Figure 5.22**). Or the cladding, in the form of a continuous membrane or expressed as a modular system of panels, may connect with but conceal the frame. In the latter case, the panel module will inevitably relate directly to the structural module (**Figure 5.23**).

The simplest method of structural expression of the frame is for the cladding to fill the void between column and beam so that structure and wall share the same plane.

Various devices have been used to express the non-structural nature of such infill like providing a glazed interface between structure

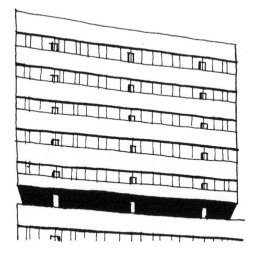

Figure 5.22 *Richard Sheppard, Robson and Partners, Science/Arts Buildings, Newcastle University, 1968. From* Architectural Review 9/68, p. 177.

and cladding so that the two systems appear visually, and therefore 'read' as, functionally separate (**Figure 5.24**).

However, the most compellingly expressive method is to locate the cladding plane well behind the structural plane so that the columns and beams visually divorced from the wall provide a 'grid' for the elevation. Within this primary order, secondary elements like shading devices can occupy the interface between structure and wall to add visual incident and scale (**Figure 5.25**).

We have already seen how architects have projected the idea of tectonic display to express not only loading and structure, but also venti-

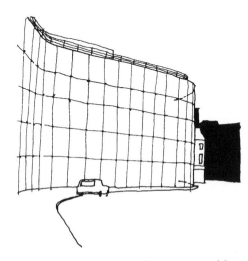

Figure 5.23 *Norman Foster, Faber Dumas Building, Ipswich, 1978.*

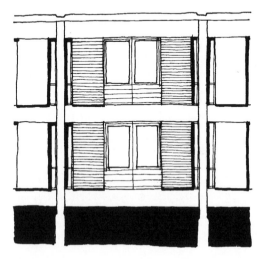

Figure 5.24 *Casson, Conder and Partners, Shopping Centre, Winchester, 1965. From* Architectural Review 2/65, p. 131.

Figure 5.25 Arup Associates, Graduate Building, Corpus Christi College, Cambridge, 1965.

Figure 5.26 Howell, Killick, Partridge and Amis, Graduate Centre, Cambridge University, 1968.

lation ducts, or movement via staircases, lifts and escalators. But many designers have sought to express not only structure but also how the entire cladding system is assembled, so that each component (and in extreme cases the actual fixings which provide their location) is revealed (**Figure 5.26**).

This is one direct method of imparting visual incident to the elevation, the end result of which equates to the practice of applying decoration, a course shunned by modernists but reinstated by their post-modern successors.

THE CORNER

The whole idea of visual intensity and how it may be achieved applies to the treatment of the 'corner'. The classical language of architecture provided several devices for celebrating the corner, and nineteenth-century eclectics delighted in applying the whole gamut of their 'free style' to augment the corner (**Figure 5.27**). Similarly freed from constraint, the so-called post-modernists have felt free to celebrate the corner, most notably at No. 1, Poultry, London, by Stirling and Wilford, 1997 (**Figure 5.28**), but also equally successfully by Terry Farrell for a modest speculative office building in Soho, London (**Figure 5.29**). In each case the density of visual event increases towards the corner.

Figure 5.27 *F. Simpson, Emerson Chambers, Newcastle upon Tyne, 1903. From* Newcastle upon Tyne, *Allsopp, B., Oriel Press.*

Figure 5.29 *Terry Farrell, Office Building, Soho, London, 1987.*

Figure 5.28 *James Stirling and Michael Wilford, No. 1 Poultry, London, 1997. From* RIBA *Journal 10/97, p. 30–31.*

Farrell uses simple means of achieving this like intensifying the fenestration pattern and introducing increasingly decorative brickwork patterns as a prelude to the corner which in each case is formed by a careful articulation of two adjacent façades. To the modernist, the idea of celebrating the corner was somewhat more problematic, but the corner and particularly the corner column, how it is fashioned and how it joins to beams, wall and roof cladding, has assumed a central importance in the appearance of framed buildings, particularly those employing an exposed steel frame (**Figures 5.30, 5.31**).

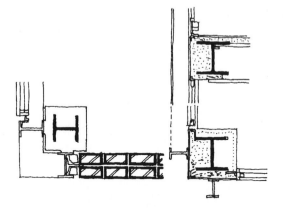

Figure 5.30 *Mies van der Rohe, Corner columns, Illinois Institute of Technology, 1946, Lake Shore Drive apartments, Chicago, 1951. From* Architecture Since 1945, *Joedecke, J., Pall Mall, p. 45.*

Figure 5.31 *David Thurlow, Eurocentre, Cambridge, 1985.*

SCALE

In this discussion of how designers can determine how their buildings look, architectural scale has been alluded to. But what do we mean by scale in the context of architectural design? Scale is not synonymous with size; even buildings of modest size can be imbued with monumental scale and vice-versa.

There exists here an analogy with the scale drawing of a building where a trained eye can accurately deduce the correct size of its constituent elements. In like fashion, the building itself possesses a 'scale' which allows us to deduce its actual physical dimensions; if that scale is 'normal', then we deduce its size correctly but increased or reduced scale misleads or confuses (either as intended by the architect or otherwise) leading to a distorted assessment of size.

Scale clues

But architectural plans, sections and elevations have a fixed scale-relationship with an observer who is interpreting them, whereas the scale-relationship between a building and an observer constantly changes as the building is approached and as more scale clues are revealed. So-called scale clues allow us to assess the size of a building by comparison with the sizes of known elements so that (either consciously or unconsciously) we learn to make judgements about a building's dimensions by constant reference to familiar elements and artefacts of known size.

These familiar elements fall into two categories. First there are general environmental elements which form the physical context for buildings, like trees and planting, vehicles, street furniture and even the occupants and users of the building (**Figure 5.32**); these are familiar objects and as environmental scale clues allow us by comparison to make some assessment of size. Second, there are familiar building elements like storey heights, masonry courses, windows, doors, and staircases which further add to our perception of a building's size (**Figure 5.33**); these are building scale

Figure 5.33 *Scale: building clues. Architects' Co-partnership, Dunelm House, Durham University, 1964.*

clues and are used by the designer to determine the scale of a building. Therefore, if these clues mislead, then we assess size incorrectly (Raskin).

Traditionally, designers working within a classical architectural language could call upon a series of familiar devices like podium, entablature, columns, and pilasters, all ordered within a strict proportioning system. But the rejection of such an architectural vocabulary by modernists during this century has been problematic as far as scale clues are concerned; an architecture embracing new structural forms with large spans and large monolithic expanses of unrelieved surfaces potentially did not offer traditional scale clues

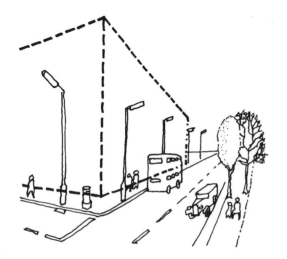

Figure 5.32 *Scale: Environmental clues.*

(**Figure 5.34**), and as we have already seen, architects were drawn to exposing structural and constructional elements to break down the building into a series of visually discrete components. In this sense, modernists have variously manipulated a tectonic display of familiar building elements to reinterpret traditional scale clues (**Figure 5.35**).

Not surprisingly, architectural scale and its potential to deceive can be a powerful tool in an architect's armoury. Therefore, architects serving totalitarian regimes have routinely harnessed monumental scale in buildings whose purpose is to symbolise temporal power (**Figure 5.36**); conversely building types such as primary schools and old people's homes consciously have been imbued with a sub-domestic scale to impart a sense of intimacy, security and wellbeing.

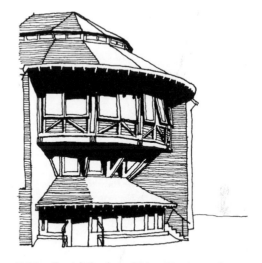

Figure 5.35   *David Thurlow, Bishop Bateman Court, Cambridge, 1985.*

Figure 5.34   *Kenzo Tange, Olympic Sports Hall, Tokyo, 1964. From* Visual History of Twentieth Century Architecture, *Sharp, D., Heinemann, p. 261.*

Figure 5.36   *Albert Speer, Great Hall, Berlin, 1941 (project).*

Depending upon the intention of the designer, scale may be manipulated in quite distinct ways which leads us to four established categories of architectural scale: normal scale, intimate scale, heroic scale and shock scale (Raskin).

Normal scale

Normal scale is the 'mean' with which the other categories compare. Most buildings we encounter are of normal scale and generally achieve this in a relaxed fashion without any self-conscious manipulation of scale clues on the part of the architect. The size of the building and its constituent parts will be precisely as perceived and anticipated by the observer. Normal scale is most readily achieved when the building looks to be broken down into a series of lesser components each of which is 'read' and contributes to a sense of visual intensity.

Intimate scale

Intimate scale, as the term suggests, is more intense than normal scale. It is achieved by reducing the size of familiar components to induce a relaxed, informal atmosphere of cosy domesticity and is applicable to building types such as old persons' housing or primary schools where a sense of comfort and security is induced by an environment of intimate scale. This can be achieved by reducing the height of window heads and cills and by reducing ceiling heights. Externally, eaves may be brought down to exaggeratedly low levels and entrance doors may be marked by canopies, all devices to increase the intensity of scale (**Figure 5.37**). Primary schools are equipped with furniture and fittings reduced in size which accentuate a sense of intimate scale. Although generous classroom ceiling heights are necessary for daylighting and ventilation, generous transoms or light shelves introduced at a lower level and broad, low internal cills are devices which may induce intimate scale (**Figure 5.38**).

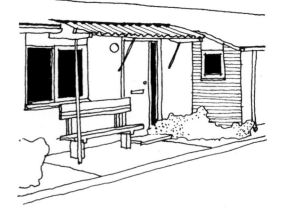

Figure 5.37 *Ralph Erskine, Housing, Killingworth, Northumberland, 1964.*

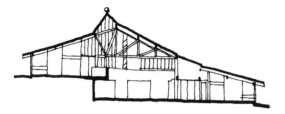

Figure 5.38 *Colin Smith, Hatch Warren Primary School, Hampshire, 1988. From* Schools of Thought, Weston, R., *Hampshire County Council.*

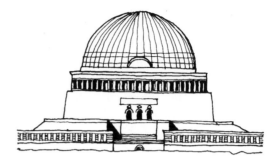

Figure 5.39 *A. N. Dushkin et al., Pantheon for heroes of the great patriotic war, 1943 (project).*

Heroic scale

Heroic scale is the converse of intimate scale in that rather than enhancing the ego of the user, it seems to diminish it. Architects have consistently used the monumentality of heroically scaled building elements as symbols of power and authority to which an individual is unable to relate his relative smallness. Therefore heroic scale has been consciously applied to a whole range of buildings which need to express their civic importance; in extreme cases like the monumental architecture of totalitarianism, architects used a stripped classical architectural language to symbolise the power of the regime but also to intimidate the users by undermining their feeling of security (**Figure 5.39**).

Vincent Harris used exactly similar methods to create an appropriate heroic scale for a range of civic buildings in pre-war Britain, many commissions being won in open competition. Typical of the genre was Sheffield City Hall completed in 1934 where Harris employed a giant Corinthian order for a huge portico mounted on a massive podium (**Figure 5.40**). Huge unrelieved areas of ashlar remove the usual scale clues to considerably enhance the scale heroically of what is a building of relatively modest dimensions. Moreover an apsidal secondary hall is elevated in scale by the surprising device of add-

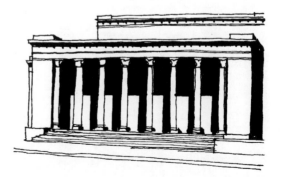

Figure 5.40 *Vincent Harris, Sheffield City Hall, 1934.*

ing a giant order of columns supporting a free-standing entablature (**Figure 5.41**).

In more recent times, architects have exploited the modernist tendency to express huge unrelieved surfaces in pursuit of heroic scale. W. M. Dudok's Hilversum Town Hall, 1930, and ironically, in its modernity pre-dating the Sheffield example, employs within a monumental De Stijl composition vast un-relieved areas of brickwork for heroic scale in a building which was to become a model for post-war civic architecture (**Figure 5.42**). Oscar Niemeyer used similarly unrelieved sur-faces but combined with massive primary Euclidean forms such as rectangular prisms which formed a cleft Secretariat tower, an

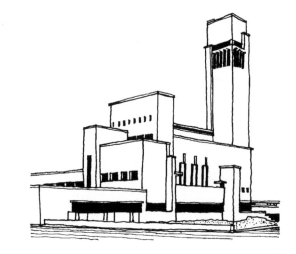

Figure 5.42   *Willem M. Dudok, Hilversum Town Hall, 1928.*

Assembly 'saucer' and a Senate 'dome' all in dramatic juxtaposition to create a governmental seat of suitably heroic scale at Brasilia in 1960 (**Figure 5.43**).

Shock scale

Shock scale is of limited use architecturally but has been put to effective use by exhibition designers or in advertising to startle and excite the observer. It depends upon familiar objects of known size being exaggeratedly expanded or reduced so that they are seen in often amus-ing scale relationships with their environment like a beer bottle hugely enlarged to serve as a brewer's dray (**Figure 5.44**). Painters like Dali

Figure 5.41   *Vincent Harris, Sheffield City Hall, 1934.*

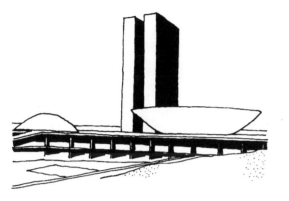

Figure 5.43 *Oscar Niemeyer, Government Buildings, Brasilia, 1960. From* Architecture Since 1945, *Joedicke, J., Pall Mall, p. 71.*

also employed the idea of shock scale for Surrealist effect.

Context

So far, we have discussed how the architect can manipulate scale to induce a pre-determined response from the user, but when designing within established contexts, particularly of a visually sensitive nature, it is important that the designer responds to the scale of that context. When Alison and Peter Smithson designed the Economist building in St. James' Street, London, 1964 (**Figure 5.45**), they not only had to respond to the scale of the existing street which one of the site boundaries addressed, but also were building on an adjacent plot to Boodle's Club, designed in 1765 by Crunden in the manner of Robert Adam. The Economist complex comprises three towers, the lowest of which addresses St. James' Street; the attic storey of the flanking towers at Boodle's is reflected in an 'attic' storey of the Economist building and Boodle's *piano nobile* is reflected

Figure 5.44 *Shock scale: Advertising. Beer wagon as beer bottle.*

Figure 5.45 *Alison and Peter Smithson, Economist Building, London, 1969.*

in the Economist's first-floor banking hall, given further prominence by its escalator access. By way of a linking device, the exposed gable of Boodle's received a faceted bay window detailed as the fenestration of the new building.

The success, therefore, of the Economist building lies in its careful response to the scale of its immediate physical context rather than in any self-conscious attempt to repeat the Palladianism of its neighbour. But in many situations the context for design is a historic building whose primacy must be maintained when extended or built alongside. Such was the case when Howell, Killick, Partridge and Amis designed the delicately-scaled senior combination room at Downing College, Cambridge, 1970, alongside the original William Wilkins building completed in 1822 (**Figures 5.46, 5.47**). The new and existing classical pavilions are linked visually by a bland screen wall which acts as a backdrop to the jewel-like senior combination room and as a neutral void between two buildings.

Figure 5.47 *Howell, Killick, Partridge and Amis, Downing College, Cambridge, Senior Combination Room, 1979.*

The wall also obscures the considerable bulk of kitchens and offices which otherwise would have upset the delicate balance of the composition. But it is the sensitive handling of scale which contributes most of this scheme's success; the primacy of Wilkins' building and its heroic scale are not undermined by the intrusion of its delicately-scaled neighbour. Moreover the new building, despite its overtly modernist tectonic display, makes subtle overtures to its classical neighbour; it sits on a 'stylobate' extended from that of the Wilkins building; the faceted pitched roof forms evoke the classical pediment next door; free-standing columns and beams give more than a hint of Wilkins' giant Ionic order and entablature.

Figure 5.46 *Howell, Killick, Partridge and Amis, Downing College, Cambridge, Senior Combination Room, 1975.*

The clear message in these two examples is that the tenets of modernism may be applied successfully to the most sensitive of contexts without recourse to historicism, often a disastrous but always a problematic course. Such was the case when Robert Venturi extended the National Gallery, London, in 1990, following a now familiar 'post-modern' response to context; the new façade echoes the neoclassicism of Wilkins' original façade (completed in 1838) but dilutes in its classical detail gradually as it recedes from the original (**Figure 5.48**). Given Venturi's skills, the contextual aims are realised, but in lesser hands, the pursuit of historicism on contextual grounds has resulted in an indescribably banal pastiche which has failed to offer a model for restoring our city streets.

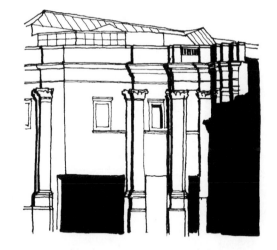

Figure 5.48   *Robert Venturi, Sainsbury Wing, National Gallery, London, 1991. From* A Celebration of Art and Architecture, *Amery, C., National Gallery (cover).*

6 THE SPACES AROUND

Our judgements of towns and cities tend to be based much more upon the nature of spaces between buildings than upon the perceived qualities of the buildings themselves. And just as there are accepted ways of form-making in the arena of architectural design, so are there accepted ways of making external spaces. The impact of new building upon existing settlements can have profound consequences if an existing urban 'grain' is not responded to sympathetically. Conversely, when establishing complexes of new buildings, it is important to establish a hierarchy of spaces between buildings which can be 'read' as clearly as that within buildings.

CENTRIFUGAL AND CENTRIPETAL SPACE

Ways of making spaces within buildings are, not surprisingly, equally applicable to establishing external spaces and a sense of enclosure induced within them. Furthermore, when considering the creation of external spaces between and around buildings, it is helpful to return to the notion of type in considering two distinct spatial types; centrifugal space and centripetal space (Ashihara).

The distinction between the two spatial types is best expressed by considering the role of the column as a spatial generator. A single column in space can define a space around it, the size of which depends upon the height of the column but the definition of which depends upon the interaction of the column and the observer (**Figure 6.1**). Therefore, a column defines a space around it in a radial fashion; this is centrifugal space.

But four columns positioned in some proximity with each other to form a 'square' will interact and induce a space enclosure (**Figure 6.2**). A centripetal order is established to define a space which even at this most basic level approximates to 'architecture without a

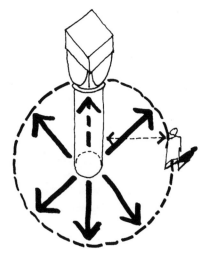

Figure 6.1 *Centrifugal space: single column.*

roof'. This is centripetal space. If four walls are used to define this centripetal space rather than four columns, then the sense of enclosure is enhanced (**Figure 6.3**), but the corners are less well defined and space tends to 'leak' from the voids thus created.

However if eight planes are used to enclose the same space by clearly defining the corners, then the perceived sense of enclosure is strengthened still further (**Figure 6.4**).

This phenomenon is best demonstrated when town 'squares' are established within the order of a town grid. If the square is formed merely by the removal of a block or blocks from the grid, then corner voids will result with a consequent loss of perceived space enclosure (**Figure 6.5**). But should the square be offset from the grid, then the corners remain intact

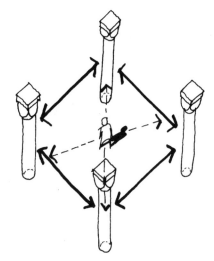

Figure 6.2 *Centripetal space: four columns.*

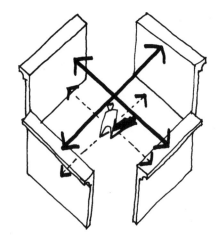

Figure 6.3 *Centripetal space: four walls.*

Figure 6.4 *Centripetal space: four corners, eight planes.*

thus heightening the sense of enclosure and giving views from the centre of the square along principal access routes (**Figure 6.6**).

As in building design, the study of precedent can provide a vital starting point for the design of spaces between buildings; whilst manifestly different in formal terms, Piazza San Marco, Venice, and Piazza del Campo, Siena have some important similarities which provide a set of clues or points of departure in the design of external centripetal spaces. First, both spaces are clearly defined as large-scale voids carved from the intense continuous grain of a city's fabric, so that they appear like public 'living rooms' without a roof, where a plethora of activities inducing social intercourse can take place.

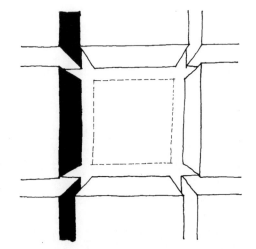

Figure 6.5 *Town square 'on grid'.*

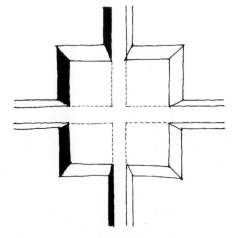

Figure 6.6 *Town square 'off grid'.*

Second, because there is no roof, the walls of the buildings which enclose the space take on great importance as primary elements within the design. Third, both spaces include a prominent vertical intervention, or campanile, as a pivotal element within the space.

The Piazza San Marco, Venice, is really two spaces in one with the free-standing campanile forming a pivot between the trapezoidal main piazza and the piazzetta. St. Mark's cathedral church addresses the tapering piazza whilst the Doge's palace and St. Mark's library contain the piazzetta's flanks, its connection with the lagoon beyond effected by the simple device of two columns forming a visual 'stop' to the piazzetta (**Figures 6.7, 6.8**). The enclosing 'walls' of the main piazza are perceived as a

Figure 6.8   *Piazzetta San Marco, Venice.*

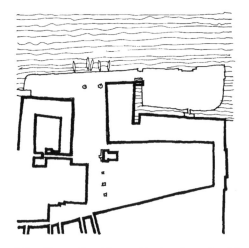

Figure 6.7   *Piazza San Marco, Venice, From* Banister Fletcher, *Architectural Press, p. 611.*

bland backdrop defining the square but also acting as a foil to the western front of the cathedral church (**Figure 6.9**). In such a context the design of the horizontal surface assumes great visual importance; this accounts for the large-scale simple geometrical paving pattern at Piazza San Marco (**Figure 6.10**).

At Piazza del Campo, Siena, the surrounding buildings also form an innocuous backdrop to the open space, but the plan is almost semi-circular with the campanile of the Palazzo del Publico at its focus. Like Venice, the paving pattern of the piazza is similarly bold with radial lines focusing on the campanile, thus linking the floorscape of the piazza and its three-dimensional form (**Figures 6.11, 6.12**).

Even such cursory analyses will reveal the importance of the enclosing walls as back-

Figure 6.9   *Saint Mark's Cathedral, Venice.*

Figure 6.11   *Siena, Piazza del Campo.*

Figure 6.10   *Piazza San Marco, Venice. Paving pattern.*

Figure 6.12   *Siena, Piazza del Campo. Paving pattern.*

ground urban architecture and how the pattern of the horizontal surface should reflect the scale of the space itself. But they also indicate that the sense of enclosure within such urban spaces is governed by the relationship between the height (H) of the buildings which define the space and the distance (D) between them. If the ratio D/H is between (1) and (4), then a satisfactory sense of enclosure will ensue; if D/H exceeds (4), then there will be insufficient interaction between the wall determinants of the space and the sense of enclosure will be lost; but should D/H be less than (1), then interaction is too great and the 'balance' of enclosure is lost (**Figure 6.13**).

This crude rule-of-thumb may be applied to significant twentieth-century developments which have hinted at new urban forms by the manipulation of centripetal space. The high-density housing development at Park Hill, Sheffield, designed by city architect, Lewis Womersley in 1960 encapsulated most of the ideas on social housing which had been formulated during the previous decade; that it is beneficial to the life of a city and to its community if a substantial provision of mixed high-density public housing is located adjacent to the city centre. This was achieved at Sheffield by manipulating a multi-storey serpentine form on a steeply-sloping site to enclose a series of public open spaces associated with the housing blocks and their high-level deck-access routes (**Figure 6.14**). But as the roof level for the entire complex remained constant, build-

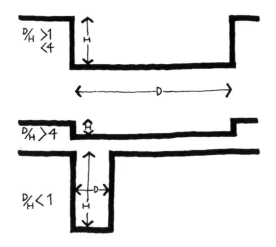

Figure 6.13 *Centripetal space enclosure, D/H ratio.*

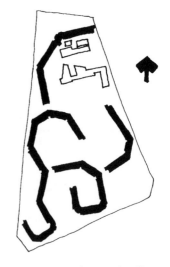

Figure 6.14 *Lewis Womersley, Park Hill Housing, Sheffield, 1961.*

ing heights decreased as the serpentine form reached the highest points of the site (**Figure 6.15**). This is reflected in the diminishing size of open spaces as the site levels rise; the smaller areas on plan respond exactly to the diminishing height of the enclosing building form, so that satisfactory D/H ratios are maintained throughout the scheme.

In 1995 Michael Hopkins used established 'centripetal' techniques to order the Inland Revenue offices in Nottingham. Here, the square and the boulevard are reinterpreted to provide public tree-lined linear spaces and enclosed private courtyards all achieved by simple attenuated building forms (**Figure 6.16**) which establish a satisfactory D/H ratio

Figure 6.15 *Lewis Womersley, Park Hill Housing, Sheffield, 1961.*

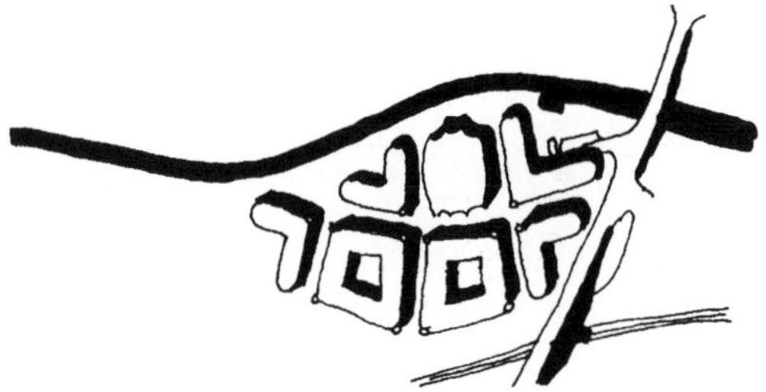

Figure 6.16 *Michael Hopkins and Partners, Inland Revenue Offices, Nottingham, 1995. From* Architectural Review 5/95.

and suggest a model for extending the city. The heart of the complex is an open public square with a jewel-like community building placed within it.

In his 1945 plan for Saint Dié, in eastern France, Le Corbusier produced a prototype for city centre development which was to be reiterated throughout war-torn Europe.

Firmly within the centrifugal category, a series of self-conscious civic buildings form a carefully placed assembly on the backdrop of an open piazza. An administrative tower block forms the visual focus and defines an open space around it.

Smaller civic buildings such as a museum and public assembly hall, interact with each other to determine the nature of the massive open public space. But essentially, the architectural devices used to achieve such open spaces are the inverse of those used in pursuit of centripetal space; now, by way of contrast, the neutral backdrop of the vertical wall is replaced by the bland horizontal surface which 'displays' a collection of architectural tours de force.

The Saint Dié model was employed by Gollins, Melvin and Ward, albeit in much diluted form, to extend the university campus at Sheffield in their competition-winning entry of 1953 (**Figure 6.17**). However, whereas Le Corbusier's plan for Saint Dié represented a symbolic rebirth of a town destroyed by war, Gollins' arrangement of rectilinear slabs and towers was extending the courtyard (centripetal) typology of a typical late Victorian British university. But the same devices emerge; a massive tower addresses the major open space and provides a visual focus for the entire campus with lower slab blocks providing a secondary rectilinear order.

The Economist Building, St. James Street, London, provides an equally potent application of centrifugal principles to urban space. Here, three towers of varying height and of similarly exquisite detailing emerge from a plaza slightly raised above the level of St. James Street (**Figures 6.18, 6.19**). The buildings, themselves raised on delicate pilotis, appear to hover over the paved plaza which again forms the backdrop to considerable architectural incident.

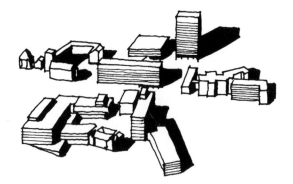

Figure 6.17 *Gollins, Melvin, Ward and Partners, Sheffield University, 1956 Master Plan. From* Britain's Changing Towns, *Nairn, I., BBC, p. 78.*

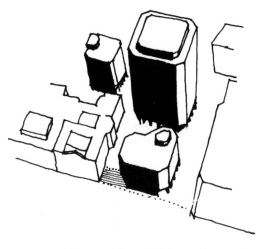

Figure 6.18 *Alison and Peter Smithson, Economist Building, London, 1965. From* The New Brutalism, *Banham, R., Architectural Press, p. 90.*

Figure 6.19 *Alison and Peter Smithson, Economist Building, London, 1965.*

URBAN SPACE TYPOLOGY

Just as the notion of 'type' may be applied to buildings (and, indeed, to the elements which constitute them, such as structure, services and cladding), so may it be applied to urban spaces. The concepts of 'centrifugal' and 'centripetal' space represent two fundamental 'types' of urban space. As already discussed, spaces around a central monument or 'figure' (centrifugal) assume the role of a backdrop or

'ground', whereas spaces enclosed by building façades (centripetal) are themselves 'figures' within a passive architectural backdrop, or 'ground' (Moughtin).

Square – enclosure

Within this framework of centrifugal and centripetal, secondary 'types' emerge, which, historically, have constituted familiar structuring elements of our towns and cities. Modernist 'centripetal' typologies reversed the accepted orthodoxy of the enclosed square, and, in the process, did not contribute significantly to its development. The traditional enclosed square (**Figure 6.20**) as a focus for social and commercial activity, as well as being the symbolic core of the community, has rarely been successfully reiterated where enclosure has been subsumed by an ill-defined open space

Figure 6.20 *Enclosed square.*

accommodating a series of free-standing architectural 'monuments' (**Figure 6.21**). But an enclosed square also imparts a sense of order, a conscious attempt to set itself apart from the chaotic nature of its hinterland, as well as being the symbolic core of the community and a focus for social and commercial activity.

As already discussed, the interaction between depth of square and height of the wall determinant creates a sense of enclosure, which is amplified if the corners of the square are clearly defined. Similar 'rules of thumb' exist for the plan form of urban squares. Sitte guarded against squares whose length was more than three times their width, Alberti championed the 'double square' where length was twice the width, whereas Vitruvius favoured a length to width ratio of 3:2.

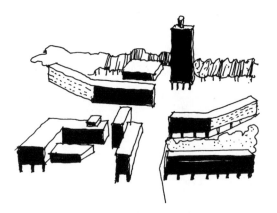

Figure 6.21 *Non-enclosed open space.*

Monument

But some squares, whilst adhering to such accepted canons, also accommodate, and are subservient to, a major civic architectural 'monument'. The urban theorist, Camillo Sitte, identified two types of square: 'deep' and 'wide'. These classifications were largely dependent upon how a major civic building addressed the square. Within the 'deep' square, the 'monument' (traditionally a church) addresses the shorter side of the square and, for maximum domination, its elevation forms the vertical determinant to one side, the other three sides being a neutral backdrop designed to accentuate the primacy of the 'monument' (**Figure 6.22**). By contrast the 'wide' square accommodates, for example, the attenuated façade of a palace to form its longer side (**Figure 6.23**), thereby dominating the other three 'neutral' elevations to the square.

Street – enclosure

Whilst the street can take on the role of the square, as a hub of social contact or commerce, it is also a route, or path, leading from one event to another. However, the latter role, in coping with ever-increasing traffic densities, has tended to obscure the street's traditional sense of 'place', where generous pavements effectively extended buildings' social spaces into the public realm.

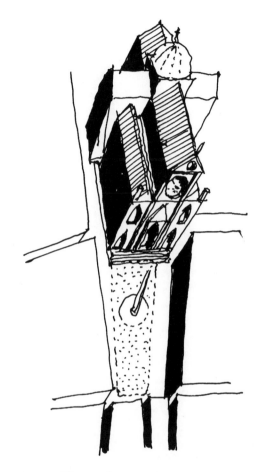

Figure 6.22 *'Short' side monument.*

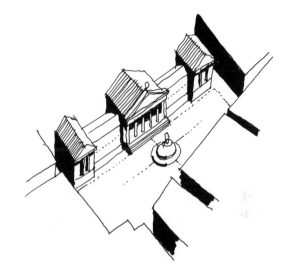

Figure 6.23 *'Long' side monument.*

The 'rules of thumb' applying to the design of squares can also be adapted to the street; a sense of enclosure depends upon the same width to height criteria, for example. But because of the street's linear form, designers have invoked various devices, not only to punctuate its length, but also to provide a satisfactory visual termination, thereby signalling entry and exit from the street as 'place'. Beaux Arts planners positioned major buildings as visual 'stops' to streets or 'boulevards' (**Figure 6.24**), and designers with 'picturesque' tendencies favoured 'setbacks' to the façade, or variations in elevational treatment and materials, as punctuations to avoid monotony (**Figure 6.25**).

Façade

Much of the characterisation of the street can be attributed to its architecture. Architects such as Robert Adam in Edinburgh's New Town,

Figure 6.24   *'Visual stop' to street.*

Figure 6.25   *'Picturesque' street.*

John Wood the elder and his son in Bath (**Figure 6.26**), or John Nash in London (**Figure 6.27**), favoured a monumental, classical architecture with repetitive bays using one material, generally dressed stone or stuccoed brick. Hence the street appeared formal and heroic in scale, characteristics quite at variance with the typically English medieval street with its informal, meandering plan, and picturesque assembly of disparate architectural forms and materials.

Figure 6.26   *The Circus, Bath.*

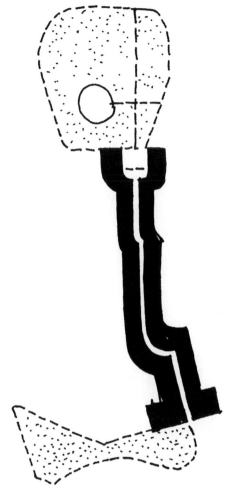

Figure 6.27 *Nash's London Plan.*

Corner

Just as architects throughout history have celebrated the corner of their buildings in a variety of ways, so have urban designers recognised the importance of the corner formed by the junction of two streets. Neo-classical stylophilists used the column to mark the corner, as did their modernist successors in their quest for structural expression. By contrast, nineteenth-century designers (and to some extent, their post-modern successors) invoked picturesque devices to intensify the corner as a visual event.

Whilst there are two generic corner types (internal and external), it is the external corner which punctuates the street and has generated its own varied typology. Thus, the designer may employ, in pursuit of formality or the picturesque ideal, angular, faceted, curved, subtractive, additive and detached corners, all offering different degrees of visual complexity (**Figures 6.28 and 6.29**).

Just as any exploration of building typology may reveal a simultaneous mix of types, even within the same building, to describe its plan, structure, or services, so too can urban space typology reveal itself as similarly pluralist.

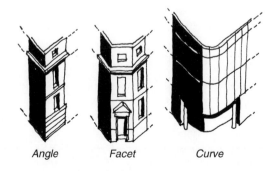

Angle   Facet   Curve

Figure 6.28 *Corner types.*

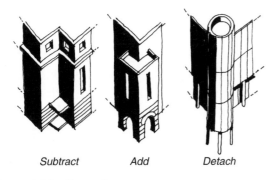

Subtract   *Add*   *Detach*

Figure 6.29   *Corner types.*

Centrifugal and centripetal space, formal and informal squares and streets enclosed by buildings of equally eclectic provenance, when employed collectively, inevitably serve to enrich the visual outcome of the wider urban domain.

7 POSTSCRIPT: A WORKING METHOD

TRADITION v. THE VIRTUAL BUILDING

Our primary concerns have been those aspects of a design programme which most profoundly influence the 'form-making' process in the prosecution of a building design. But having established a 'form' which meets the major design objectives and is capable of development, this process represents in time but a fraction of the entire protracted design period. Nevertheless, it represents by far the most crucial (and arguably, the most problematic) activity for the designer; flawed decisions in form-making cannot be retrieved by subsequent assiduous attention to detail but only appropriate formal responses at this stage can form the basis of meaningful architecture. Moreover, they can be developed to enhance the clarity of that initial concept.

And which techniques are most appropriate for prosecuting and developing the design at this early conceptual stage? As we enter the twenty-first century, the enormous sophistication of computer software for drafting and three-dimensional modelling has fundamentally altered the traditional view that a soft pencil and tracing paper, supported by physical models in cardboard or balsa wood, are the best tools to facilitate our initial, tentative, form-making excursions.

Design by drawing

Nevertheless, it is axiomatic that a facility for drawing most emphatically assists the design process; 'design by drawing', then, represents by far the most accessible and efficient method for early exploration in design. Moreover, overlays of tracing paper, because of their transparency, allow swift modification of an initial 'form' again and again without having to repeat the whole process from scratch; the results of this process can then be assessed by means of a physical model. Even at this stage, coloured pencils can be used, 'coding' drawings to distinguish spatial hierarchies. Such clarity will help not only the ongoing assessment of the emerging design's validity, but will also assist in maintaining the clarity of the diagram as the design develops.

Designs cannot be 'tested' until they are drawn to scale. Only in this way can the designer 'feel' the size of building elements in relation to each other and in relation to the site and its physical context. A range of appropriate preferred scales should be used which will vary according to the size of the project but it is essential that as many aspects of the design as possible are developed concurrently. Having established a 'diagram' to scale, details of major junctions can be explored at larger scale, so building up as early as possible a comprehensive picture of design intent. It is useful to retain evidence of these early sketches as a design 'log' so that, if necessary, rejected solutions can be revisited and reassessed as the design progresses; this may form a useful reference, particularly if drawn on sheets of standard-size, numbered and dated.

At the same time it is imperative to build up a fact-file for reference on precedent studies of comparable building types, appropriate structural systems, construction, materials and environmental performance.

Architects conceive and design their buildings from the outset as three-dimensional artefacts and, as already indicated, a facility for drawing greatly facilitates such conceptual-isation. In these early stages therefore, it is imperative to develop freehand axonometric and perspective drawing methods which can quickly explore the three-dimensional consequences of design decisions.

The virtual building

Although it is now unthinkable that fledgling architects could enter their profession without sophisticated levels of computer literacy, nevertheless, there is still a perception amongst many that hand drawing and physical models offer a more direct and flexible design tool than computer-generated techniques. But if the central role of the architect is to create spaces for human habitation, then it seems axiomatic that the virtual building, which provides an accurate three-dimensional representation of the designer's concept, will allow him to understand the project more comprehensively.

Essentially, the virtual building is an accurately described digital representation of an architectural design modelled three-dimensionally. As the project develops, the virtual building allows the architect to accurately 'test' the three-dimensional outcomes of design decisions that affect the nature of external form, internal space, and junctions of components. Moreover, because it is represented by one model, then the need to co-ordinate several drawings is removed, and the margin for error, inherent in traditional methods, is therefore substantially reduced. Two-dimensional plans, sections and elevations may also be extracted for evaluation early in the design process, with any modifications subsequently being fed back into the single virtual building model.

Whereas with 'design by drawing', early decisions regarding planning, structure, and construction, for example, will accelerate the design process, with the virtual building, such decisions must be logged into a database at an early stage for the design to proceed at all. In the event, this not only represents good practice, but also allows the three-dimensional model to provide a complete visualisation of the project, which can then be communicated, electronically, to other members of the design team.

The virtual building, in effect, offers a new *method* of designing buildings by offering instant evaluation of the project in two and three-dimensional images at any stage of the design process, a process of refinement which, by comparison, traditional drawing renders unacceptably labour-intensive.

The purpose of this book has been to establish a sensible working method for getting the massively complex process of designing a building under way, for inevitably it is within these early decisions and tentative forays into form-making that the seeds of true architecture are sown. And yet it represents a mere beginning, for design activity carries on until the building is completed on site: reordering may well ensue during a building's 'first life' and beyond should recycling of salvaged building components be considered in the original design. It is not within our scope here to chart that entire process; more to suggest that its effectiveness will inevitably depend upon this initial exploration of uncharted territory in search of an appropriate 'form'.

But that exploration could also heed Albert Einstein's sage counsel; 'If you wish to learn from the theoretical physicist anything about the methods he uses ... don't listen to his words, examine his achievements.' The same could well apply to architecture.

FURTHER READING

Abel, C., *Architecture and Identity; Towards a Global Eco-culture*, Architectural Press, 1997.

Ashihara, Y., *Exterior Design in Architecture*, Van Nostrand Reinhold, 1970.

Banham, R., *The Age of the Masters; a Personal View of Modern Architecture*. Architectural Press, 1975.

Banham, R., *The Architecture of the Well-tempered Environment*, Architectural Press, 1969.

Blanc, A., *Stairs, Steps and Ramps*, Architectural Press, 1996.

Brawne, M., *From Idea to Building*, Architectural Press, 1992.

Broadbent, G., *Design in Architecture*; John Wiley and Sons, 1973.

Chilton, J., *Space Grid Structures*, Architectural Press, 2000.

Cook, P., *Primer*, Academy Editions, 1996.

Curtis, W., *Modern Architecture since 1900*, Phaidon, 1982.

Edwards, B., *Sustainable Architecture*, Architectural Press, 1996.

Edwards, B., *Rough Guide to Sustainability*, RIBA Publications, 2002.

Groak, S., *The Idea of Building*, E&F Spon, 1992.

Hawkes, D., *The Environmental Tradition*, E. and F. N. Spon, 1996.

Howes, J., *Computers Count*, RIBA Publications, 1990.

Hunt, A., *Tony Hunt's Structures Notebook*, Architectural Press, 1997.

Jencks, C., *Modern Movements in Architecture*, Penguin Books, 1973.

Lawson, B., *How Designers Think*, Architectural Press, 1998.

Lawson, B., *Design in Mind*, Architectural Press, 1994.

MacDonald, A., *Structure and Architecture*, Architectural Press, 1994.

Moughtin, C., *Urban Design: Street and Square*, Architectural Press, 1992.

Moughtin, C. et al., *Urban Design; Method and Techniques*, Architectural Press, 1999.

Porter, T., Goodman, S., *Design Drawing Techniques for Architects, Graphic Designers and Artists*, Architectural Press, 1992.

Raskin, E., *Architecturally Speaking*, Bloch Publishing Co., 1997.

Sharp, D., *A Visual History of Twentieth-century Architecture*, Heinemann, 1972.

Smith, P., *Options for a Flexible Planet*, Sustainable Building Network, Sheffield, 1996.

Smith, P., *Architecture in a Climate of Change*, Architectural Press, 2001.

Sparke, P., *Design in Context*, Guild Publishing, 1987.

Tutt, P., Adler, D. (eds), *New Metric Handbook: Planning and Design Data*, Architectural Press, 1979.

Vale, B., Vale, R., *Green Architecture: Design for a Sustainable Future*, Thames and Hudson, 1991.

Wilson, C., *Architectural Reflections*, Architectural Press, 1992.